Contents

Foreword

The publication of Dr. Wong-Diaz's monograph coincides with a major strategic reassessment of U.S. national security interests and future military posture taking place at the national level. Driven by the end of Operation New Dawn, the last phase of the Iraq War, and the impending withdrawal of U.S. forces from Afghanistan, this reassessment considers both the desired international role of the United States and the military posture needed to secure U.S. interests. At the same time, politically mobilized populations have brought sweeping change to the Middle East and North Africa, creating security challenges that cannot be met solely through conventional military means. Indeed, the strategic environment the U.S. finds itself in today requires astute statecraft to formulate and execute grand strategy, a concept Dr. Wong-Diaz explores in depth.

For the last 10 years the United States has projected its national power primarily through large-scale troop deployment in major contingency operations in Iraq and Afghanistan. At the time of the 9/11 attacks, the United States was indisputably the world's super power, able to exert dominant influence across the globe. There were few challenges to the nation's economic and conventional military strength.

A decade later, the U.S. position in the world has changed dramatically. Though the United States remains the world's largest economy and retains unparalleled military capability, very high levels of debt undermine America's global stature. In 2010, Admiral Mike Mullen, then Chairman of the Joint Chiefs of Staff, declared the national debt to be the most severe threat to national security, undermining U.S. capability to act. Indeed, attempts to reign in the national debt will require deep cuts in defense spending. Under the current budget request to Congress the U.S. Department of Defense will reduce spending by $487 billion over the next 10 years, a 20 percent decrease from 2010 levels.

To pursue its global interests in an era characterized by austerity, the United States will need to draw on all of its tools of statecraft—including diplomatic, economic, psychological, and subversive—as well as military means. The term "hard power" often refers to conventional military force, economic sanctions, and other coercive means, including diplomacy. 'Soft power' is the ability to influence others to act in ways that achieve one's goals. To achieve its goals the United States must conduct strategies that effectively blend all forms of power and uses them smartly to achieve its goals. Though there is no agreement on what constitutes smart use of U.S. power, the concept of "smart power" is a dominant theme in policy circles.

Smart power, however defined, is directly relevant to the SOF community. With a smaller footprint than conventional forces, SOF are both a cost-effective and less visible instrument of national power. Moreover, SOF warriors are '3-D' warriors, skilled in diplomacy, development, and defense, and expected to combine both 'hard' and 'soft' power approaches instinctively to achieve strategic level effects. Using case studies from around the world, Dr. Wong-Diaz's monograph expertly draws the links between the strategic level projection of power by states and their consequences on the ground. Undoubtedly this monograph will spark significant debate for years to come.

Kenneth H. Poole, Ed.D.
Director, JSOU Strategic Studies Department

About the Author

D r. Francisco Wong-Diaz is a senior fellow with the Joint Special Operations University Strategic Studies Department. A naturalized American citizen, he is emeritus of international affairs and law at the City College of San Francisco and expert subject lecturer at the U.S. Air Force Special Operations School and JSOU. A member of the Global Futures Forum, he was an academic fellow on terrorism with the Foundation for the Defense of Democracies (2007). Previously he was a fellow at the University of California (UC) at the Berkeley Center for the Teaching and Study of American Cultures (1995); visiting scholar and research associate at UC Berkeley Graduate School of Business (1983); visiting researcher at the Hoover  Institution (1971); and Rackham fellow in political science at the University of Michigan (1967 to 1970). He has taught at the University of Michigan (1967 to 1969), University of Detroit (1967), and San Francisco State University (1977) and presented at Columbia University School of Law, Stanford University, The University of Texas, University of Southern California, University of Miami (Florida), and others. His interest areas include U.S. foreign policy, strategy, counterterrorism, intelligence, national security law, and Cuban and Latin American politics.

Dr. Wong-Diaz is an active member of the State Bar of California (1980), the Florida Bar (1987), and the U.S. District Court for the Northern District of California (1981). A former research assistant to the Honorable Frank Newman, Associate Justice of the California Supreme Court (1976 to 1977), and law clerk of the presiding judge of Marin County Superior Court (1980), he served on the editorial boards of the *California Lawyer* (1991 to 1994), the *Industrial Relations Law Journal* (1975 to 1976), and the *Ecology Law Quarterly* (1976). A U.S. Department of State diplomat/scholar (1975), he served as dean/director of the Inter-American Center at Miami-Dade College (1985 to 1986); special assistant to the chancellor (1984 to 1985) and chairman of Latin American Studies/Coordinator of Legal Studies at the City College of San Francisco (1979 to 1985).

Recent major publications include *Castro's Cuba: Quo Vadis?* (Strategic Studies Institute, U.S. Army War College, December 2006) and *American Politics in a Changing World* (2004 revision). His articles, commentary, and op-editions have also appeared in *The New York Times, San Jose Mercury News, Washington Times, Marin Independent Journal, Hispanic Magazine Online, FrontPage* magazine, and elsewhere. For over two decades he has provided political analysis and news commentary in Spanish for Univisión and guest appeared on nationally broadcast radio PBS, NBC News, CBS, and other media outlets.

Dr. Wong-Diaz is listed in *Who's Who in America, Who's Who in the World*, and *Who's Who in American Law.* Memberships include the Pacific Council on International Policy, American Bar Association (Standing Committee on Law and National Security), International Institute for Strategic Studies, Proteus U.S. Army War College, Committee on the Present Danger, the Association for the Study of the Middle East and Africa, Commonwealth Club, and the World Association of International Studies. He was recognized as one of the "100 most influential Hispanics in the nation" by *Hispanic Business* magazine.

He received his B.A. in Political Science (1965) from Northern Michigan University, M.A. in Social Science (1967) from the University of Detroit, M.A. in Political Science (1970) and Ph.D. in Political Science (1974) from the University of Michigan, and Juris Doctor from UC-Berkeley School of Law (Boalt Hall, 1976). He specialized in national security law at the University of Virginia School of Law Center for National Security Law (1996) and in trial advocacy at UC-Hastings College of the Law (1995).

1. American Power in Decline?

The dissolution of the Union of Soviet Socialist Republics (USSR) in 1991 generated a hopeful mood throughout the Western world as the Cold War ended, leaving the United States as the sole superpower. The unipolar era that followed did not bring lasting peace, however, but global uncertainty and persistent conflict. In a short period of time, the mood in the "lonely superpower"[1] faded in the face of the terrorist attacks on 11 September 2001, the wars that followed in Afghanistan and Iraq, and the deepest global economic crisis since the 1930s global depression. The U.S. and its allies currently face daunting challenges and threats including violent extremists, cyber war, nuclear proliferation, nuclear terrorism, integrated terrorist networks and transnational criminal organizations, failed or failing states, a resurgent authoritarian Russia, humanitarian crises, China's rise, and the "rise of the rest."[2]

In this increasingly complex global security environment, the concept of national security itself is said to comprise a myriad of components such as energy, information systems, demographic and climatic restiveness, mineral resources, food, water, and sociopolitical disorders associated with globalization and issues of governance.[3] As the United States reduced its military footprint in Iraq and U.S.-North Atlantic Treaty Organization (NATO) operations continued in Afghanistan, the demographically driven turmoil of the "Arab Spring" spread along the "arc of instability" spanning from North Africa across the Middle East to the Indian Ocean. In these conflict areas, Special Operations Forces (SOF), with their innate capabilities, skill sets, and a force structure exceptionally suited to engage the diverse, networked, technologically savvy, asymmetric adversaries, have been at the tip of the spear.[4]

Meanwhile, the center of gravity for global power has shifted from the West to Asia to such an extent that the International Monetary Fund announced that the "Age of America" would pass by the year 2016 when the People's Republic of China (PRC), with an annual growth rate of 9.7 percent, would become the world's largest economy and the most rapidly modernizing military power.[5] This accelerated geopolitical transformation is becoming a major priority for United States strategic planners long preoccupied by the war against violent extremists.

This confluence of events revived the 1970s Vietnam War era debate about America's decline and ability to maintain its global leadership position.[6] The question being asked is whether the U.S. would any longer be "bound to lead" in a multipolar world for lacking not only the will but the capacity to lead.[7] In his 1996 declaration of war against the U.S., Osama bin Laden concluded that our retreat from Lebanon, Yemen, and Somalia were signs of decline—"God has dishonored you when you withdrew, and it clearly showed your weaknesses and powerlessness."[8] Likewise, a Communist Chinese study on "American social diseases" identified social problems like homelessness, racial gaps, extremism, family breakdown, crime and drug use, and spiritual and moral crises as internal weaknesses that would bring about America's decline.[9] Former President Bill Clinton told an audience in a 2002 speech in Australia: "This is a unique moment in U.S. history, a brief moment, history, when the U.S. has preeminent military, economic, and political power. It won't last forever. This is just a period, a few decades this will last."[10] More recently, the influential *Foreign Policy* magazine carried the headline "American Decline—This Time It's Real."[11]

Joseph Nye, former assistant secretary of defense and former dean of Harvard's Kennedy School of Government, distinguishes between two dimensions of decline—absolute and relative. Absolute decline refers to a sense of decay while relative decline sees the power resources of other states grow or be used more effectively. In his view, the U.S. is challenged with absolute decline in areas of debt, secondary education, and political gridlock, and relative decline in rate of economic growth.[12] In contrast, some deny the decline and argue that despite complex challenges and perceptions (or misperceptions) of decline, "American leadership is still the global norm,"[13] the apparent decline is just a "return to normalcy,"[14] or that the appearance of decline is a function of the "rise of the rest in a post-American world."[15] Others advocate that we should strive to preserve our dominant position in a unipolar world system.[16] To another set of analysts, America's decline as a superpower is creating a multipolar world in which the U.S. will be "primus inter pares" (first among equals).[17]

A recent comparison of the United States with the rest of the world on an index of several variables or drivers (e.g. general welfare of the population, common defense, blessings of liberty) indicates that the U.S. remains the world's largest economy ($14 trillion per year) with a high per capita income ($41,000); while China, despite its rapid transformation, has an average income per capita of just $6,000 or just half of that of Mexico and Turkey. The U.S. still has the world's largest military, and its defense spending as a percentage of gross domestic products (GDP) increased slightly. Meanwhile, China replaced Russia as the second-largest military based on spending.[18] One concern is the reliability of Chinese defense budget data given the lack of transparency of their system. Less encouraging were the economists attending their annual convention who generally foretold U.S. decline and China's ascension as the world's largest economy. One attendee even confirmed the aforementioned prediction in the Chinese "social diseases" study that:

> The United States will need to come to terms with the fact that its prevalence in the world is fated to come to an end … This will be difficult for many Americans to swallow and the United States should brace for social unrest amid blame over who was responsible for squandering global primacy.[19]

The traditional U.S. military capability remains unmatched, but it might be degraded and compromised because, as former Chairman of the Joint Chiefs of Staff Admiral Mike Mullen warned, "Our national debt is our biggest national security threat."[20] Former Secretary of State Hillary Clinton echoed the concern by calling the 2010 U.S. deficit a "message of weakness internationally" that poses a national security threat in two ways: "it undermines our capacity to act in our own interest, and it does constrain us where constraint may be undesirable."[21]

On 28 February 2011, the Total Public Debt Outstanding of the United States of America of $14.19 trillion was 96.8 percent of calendar year 2010's annual GDP of $14.66 trillion.[22] Former Secretary of Defense Robert M. Gates, seeking to balance military operations and the challenge of new competitors and adversaries, sought to reduce defense spending while still fighting wars in Iraq and Afghanistan. With federal tax cuts extended for two years and the widespread opposition to tax increases in the midst of the worst recession since the Great Depression of the 1930s, Gates's plan was to effect "efficiency savings" that would slow the defense budget's rate of growth and transform not only the way America prepares for and fights wars, but also how the military industrial complex does business.[23] Consequently, within the past few years, dozens of weapons programs were cut, and in May 2011 Secretary Gates issued a directive to attain $100 billion in savings spread over a five-year period to safeguard a yearly growth of about 1 percent in defense spending. By so proposing, however, he soon came under criticism for not cutting enough[24] or, on the other hand, for cutting too much and "re-hollowing the military."[25]

Secretary Gates appeared to have lost an administration internal budget dispute as the White House directed the Pentagon to reduce its budget by $78 billion over the next five years. Thus, on 6 January 2011, he announced that the nation's "extreme fiscal duress" required him to affect cuts in the size of the Army and Marine Corps. It would be the first decrease in the Department of Defense (DOD) budget since 1998 and the first troop cuts in decades. The White House decision seemed to have come as a surprise, for American troops continued to engage in Iraq and the Afghanistan/Pakistan areas amidst growing concern in military circles about the intentions behind China's accelerated growth and modernization of its military capabilities.[26]

On 14 February 2011, President Barack Obama sent Congress a $671 billion 2012 defense spending plan, including $117.8 billion for the wars in Iraq and Afghanistan and $13 billion in program cancellations. This request came as Congress debated the fiscal year (FY) 2011 budget. For FY 2012, the DOD's record base operating budget request of about $553 billion would be $22 billion above the level for 2010.[27] The Pentagon would thereafter seek in the out years estimated spending equivalent to $571 billion in 2013, $586 billion in 2014, $598 billion in 2015, and $611 billion by 2016. House Armed Services Committee Chairman Representative Howard McKeon expressed significant concerns about this budget plan because it "leads to zero percent real growth in the out years" since in order to meet increasing salary, health care, fuel costs, and avoid program cuts, the DOD needs a 2-3 percent annual increase.[28] While some commentators viewed the budget as an indication that the "Pentagon's buying power is in decline,"[29] others considered the cuts a step in the right direction that "If anything, doesn't go far enough."[30]

As a point of comparison, the PRC had a 2010 defense budget of 532.115 billion yuan (approximately U.S. $86.5 billion at current exchange rates) or an increase of 7.5 percent more than the previous year but down from the 14.9 percent increase in 2009. China's defense budget has increased by a whopping 12.9 percent annually since 1989. Yet compared to the $600 billion plus budget the U.S. is due to spend, China's military spending still remains substantially lower.[31] The task of achieving a "leaner and meaner defense," however, cannot be delayed.[32] For example, as part of the far reaching budget cuts in the Pentagon, the U.S. Joint Forces Command closed with a loss of thousands of jobs in Virginia and a couple hundred at MacDill Air Force Base in Tampa, Florida, saving about $420 million.[33] Despite these efforts, however, the American intervention in the Libyan conflict and the humanitarian aid mission in Japan's post-tsunami nuclear crisis will affect defense budget estimates. In fact, on 13 April 2011 President Obama proposed to reduce the budget deficit by $4 trillion over a 10-year period. To accomplish this goal, "we're going to have to conduct a fundamental review of America's missions, capabilities, and our role in a changing world" in order to reduce defense spending by $400 billion by 2023, he said.[34] Though the exact extent of defense budget cuts over the next decade are not yet determined, it is clear that there will be a significant reduction in spending and reprioritization of effort.

Faced with unabated tensions with North Korea and Iran over their nuclear programs, former Defense Secretary Gates had sought a restoration of military-to-military exchanges with China. As the national debate shifted from ends and means in the fight against threats to the United States to the economy and costs, the DOD sought to adjust to the budgetary realities. While affirming that global terrorism cannot be defeated by hard military might alone, Gates openly lamented the withering of diplomatic capacity and the resulting militarization of American foreign policy asking for a rebalancing of missions and programs so the U.S. military will become more efficient and focused.[35] Against this backdrop, the study will explore relevant issues and debates associated with statecraft and the calls for rebalancing. Pressing issues in an era of economic austerity demand the exercise of the highest level of statecraft and strategic vision to guarantee the security and survival of the American nation in a multipolar or multinodal world, to use the terminology of the most recent National Military Strategy.[36] The study is concerned with how conceptualizations about the global security environment affect the use of U.S. power in response to the threats and challenges the United States faces, or might face, in the future. The tenor of the study is thematically more strategy, statecraft, and policy assessment than operational and tactical in nature.

Arguably, since the end of the Cold War the United States has lacked a comprehensive and cohesive overarching organizing principle or grand strategy that prioritizes goals, identifies means, and applies the proper tools of power to guide the United States through the geopolitical challenges of the first half of the 21st century.[37] As a result, crucial decisions regarding war and peace are made on an ad hoc, muddling-through basis with mixed results at a significant cost in lives and treasure. The failings of international relations theory, the unmatched role of key individuals in developing and implementing a grand strategy of containment for the Cold War, and issues of statecraft are relevant contributing factors in maintaining this general condition.

As the international order grew in complexity and the U.S. became its guarantor, the special operations community operating at the tip of the spear assumed the role of global first responders.

The Greek historian Thucydides wrote that nations went to war out of "fear, honor, or interest,"[38] and Prussia's military theorist Carl Von Clausewitz in a famous aphorism defined war as a political activity: "War is not merely a political act, but also a political instrument, a continuation of political relations, a carrying out of the same by other means."[39] For John G. Stoessinger, in war a leader's perception of himself, his adversary's character, his adversary's intentions, his perceptions of the adversary's power and capabilities, and his capacity for empathy with his adversary are all extremely important.[40] This study seeks to move through the levels of analysis (global, domestic, individual) in a nonlinear fashion while focusing attention on the debates and individual actors who determine or influence when, where, and how warriors engage in war.[41] Leaders are important because, as retired Army General Stanley McChrystal said, "That's how you succeed. That's how you win in war, that's how you win in politics, that's how you win in just about everything."[42] Not only leaders of the nation matter, but their advisers, generals, and statesmen, too.[43] President John F. Kennedy once said to Annapolis graduates:

> You military professionals must know something about strategy and tactics and logistics, but also economics and politics and diplomacy and history. You must know everything you can know about military power, and you must also understand the limits of military power.

> You must understand that few of the important problems of our time have ... been finally solved by military power alone.[44]

SOF are tasked to implement the most difficult missions based on national policymakers' perspectives and policy preferences. As SOF seek to operate "ahead of the sound of the guns," they heed President Kennedy's call to understand what is happening in the world so they can best prepare, adapt, and innovate to fulfill those missions.[45] Just as policymakers need to be aware of the SOF Truths that "humans are more important than hardware" and "SOF warriors cannot be mass-produced,"[46] so do military leaders and operators need to know "the political realities that govern military operations."[47] This study is a step in that journey of discovery to educate SOF as we address questions such as: What is statecraft? How do conceptualizations about "hard, soft, and smart" power affect the pursuit of national security interests? What is the nature of the debate about a balanced strategy and warfare?

This paper will focus on the previous set of questions and examine contemporary efforts at statecraft by examining the conceptions of hard, soft, and smart power. This paper will also look at the new Solarium movement and briefly note the debates over counterinsurgency (COIN). Finally, an examination of the issues associated with balancing strategy and warfare will be discussed.

2. Statecraft and Power

Literary insight is essential for statecraft – Charles Hill[48]

What is "statecraft?" Why is it so important? The term statecraft has longevity, but there is no general agreement on its specific meaning. One simple but unsatisfactory definition equates it with governing: Statecraft is the "art of conducting state affairs."[49] Statecraft is not the same as "governing," which is the administration and organization of a political entity. Daniel Drezner's course on the "Art and Science of Statecraft" at Tufts University seeks "to offer an introduction into the world of policymaking, diplomacy, and statecraft," thus suggesting that statecraft is the crafting and implementing of foreign policy.

A "remedial primer" defines statecraft as an instrumentality, or how states may use prestige, diplomacy, economics, subversion, and force to serve their ends.[50] Veteran diplomat Chas W. Freeman has described the meaning and practice of statecraft in more vivid terms:

> Statecraft translates national interests and concerns into national goals and strategies. It is the strategy of power. It guides the ways the state deploys and applies its power abroad. These ways embrace the arts of war, espionage, and diplomacy. The practitioners of these three arts are the paladins of statecraft. The military are the fists of statecraft. Espionage is the sixth sense of the state. Spies are statecraft's hidden eyes, ears, and hands. Diplomats are statecraft's visible eyes, ears, and hands. They are the voice of their state in foreign lands. Diplomacy is the form that statecraft takes in times of peace.[51]

Freeman wisely counsels the need to continue diplomatic dialogue or statecraft even when coercion replaces persuasion as a means of influence. Indeed, while Jessica Glicken Turnley sees war and diplomacy at opposite ends of a force-persuasion continuum,[52] diplomatic activity by valiant souls has continued under extreme circumstances during wartime, as shown by the World War II examples of "savior diplomats" like Swedish diplomat Raoul Wallenberg and Mexican Gilberto Bosques.[53] Economic activities (e.g. assets seizures, currency, export controls, import bans, subsidies boycotts, embargoes) and information must also be given equal billing as tools of statecraft.[54] Dennis Ross, State Department Director of Policy Planning under George H.W. Bush, sees statecraft in broad terms as "knowing how best to integrate and use every asset or military, diplomatic, intelligence, public, economic, or psychological tool we possess (or can manipulate) to meet our objectives."[55]

Ross believes that "good" statecraft involves "developing aims and strategies that fit both the context and the means available," thereby identifying statecraft with the proper shaping and managing of an overarching or grand strategy. "Bad" statecraft, on the other hand, "creates mismatches between means and ends."[56] Left unanswered is whether good statecraft can be practiced in the absence of a grand strategy.

The art of statecraft, though at times confused with diplomacy, amounts to the holistic use of diplomacy, military capabilities, economic resources, intelligence sources, information systems, and cultural tools by a political entity for strategic purposes.[57] As Kaplan noted, "statecraft includes the construction of strategies for securing the national interest in the international arena, as well as the execution of these strategies."[58] Great power statecraft seeks to formulate and execute grand strategy.

Tools of Statecraft: Hard, Soft, and Smart Power

In order to best understand current challenges to the U.S. practice of statecraft, it is therefore necessary to delve into the current debates about hard, soft, and smart power. The reason being that the "first principle of grand strategy is that one must understand what is going on in the world"[59] so that statecraft may follow from such an assessment. The immediate task ahead is therefore to answer the fundamental question—what is happening?

A trinity of "hard, soft, and smart power" catchwords has entered the political lexicon in recent years regarding the nature, composition, and use of the toolbox of statecraft. Classical realists, as mentioned earlier, emphasized the role of military force as the main instrument of power in international relations due to the centrality of war. A nation's power was a function of its ability to defend itself and its friends from aggression and conquest through military means. In a global arena characterized by a self-help system, developing and maintaining military capabilities or forming alliances with those who had them was critical in order to survive the power struggle. Great power status in turn was conferred by "strength for war."[60]

During World War II, Soviet dictator Joseph Stalin, talking with British Prime Minister Winston Churchill in 1944, asked, "How many divisions does the Pope of Rome have?" Later, hearing about Stalin's query, Pope Pius XII responded, "You can tell my son Joseph that he will meet my divisions in heaven."[61] Stalin's statement reflected the mindset of what Joseph Nye Jr. calls hard power leadership while the Pope's response made reference to his soft power. Nye, a liberal advocate of complex interdependence theory, coined the term "soft power" in a 1990 book arguing that there are two types of power: "hard" and "soft." The use of hard power is associated with realist and neorealist thinking and their strategic reliance on military force, economic sanctions, and coercive diplomacy as instruments of statecraft.[62] For example, Otto von Bismarck, a hard power practitioner, became known as the Iron Chancellor after he declared, "This policy cannot succeed through speeches, and shooting matches, and songs; it can be only be carried out through blood and iron."[63] Hard power is command power based on economic and military tools, and it is measured by such tangibles as population, military assets, GDP, natural resources, political stability, and so on.

Soft power is defined as indirect or co-optive power behavior, the ability to get what you want by attracting and persuading others to adopt your goals. Soft power is the power of "attraction" as opposed to the power of coercion or payment.[64] A country's soft power could come from three sources: its culture, political values, and its foreign policies.[65] The official instruments of soft power include public diplomacy, broadcasting, military-to-military contacts, exchange programs, development assistance, and disaster relief. [66] Huntington agreed with Nye on the increased diffusion of power throughout the world but then asked, "What makes culture and ideology attractive?" For him, Nye's soft power is "power only when it rests on a foundation of hard power."[67] In response to criticism, Nye reaffirmed that the distinction between soft and hard power is one of degree and that soft power is also a key element of leadership albeit hard to use due to its limitations.[68]

Military prowess and competence can sometimes create soft power. Osama bin Laden allegedly said people are attracted to a strong horse rather than a weak horse.[69] A well-run military can be a source of admiration in some countries while misuse of military resources can also undercut soft power.[70] Stalin's cult of personality and ruthless "Great Terror" with an estimated death toll of 20 million people could be an attractive model to emulate by aspiring totalitarian leaders.[71]

The term soft power is but a new rendition of an old set of political concepts. Use of information and means of communication to persuade, influence, and attract has been a defining characteristic of diplomacy and political propaganda for a long time. In colonial times, American patriots led by Samuel Adams organized Committees of Public Correspondence to achieve unity by keeping the public informed about political development and instigating public outrage against the British Stamp Act and Townshend duties in the 1760s. By the time of the American Revolution, the committees had become "a powerful political weapon for revolutionary action."[72] One of the most famous colonial figures is Boston silversmith Paul Revere who made approximately 20 rides as a special courier carrying dispatches for the Boston Committee of Correspondence between December 1773 and November 1775.[73]

The United States Committee on Public Information (CPI), known as the Creel Committee after George Creel its chairman, was created in April 1917 after the U.S. declared war on Germany. Creel defined the committee's work as an advertising campaign about American ideals and the purpose of the war effort.[74] To attain that purpose, the CPI produced millions of copies of booklets for domestic and foreign distribution and sent thousands of speakers to meet the public.[75]

Soft power became so popular in the last two decades in academia and elements of the foreign policy establishment that it has been called "one of the most successful neologism of the last two decades."[76] In particular, after the release of the 2006 Iraq Study Group Report, it gave pause to those who emphasized military solutions to political problems and was propounded as an alternative to the use of force as a tool of statecraft.[77] The U.S. Army, moving toward the new paradigm of nation-building or "stability operations" in failing states, embraced soft power in *Field Manual 3-07 Stability Operations*:

> America's future abroad is unlikely to resemble Afghanistan or Iraq, where we grapple with the burden of nation-building under fire. Instead, we will work through and with the community of nations to defeat insurgency, assist fragile states, and provide vital humanitarian aid to the suffering. Achieving victory will assume new dimensions as we strengthen to generate soft power to promote participation in government, spur economic development,

and address the root causes of conflict among the disenfranchised population of the world.[78]

Despite soft power's liberal origins, its proponents are found in both major parties. In the second term of the George W. Bush administration, then Defense Secretary Robert Gates endorsed it in a Landon Lecture:

> One of the most important lessons of the wars in Iraq and Afghanistan is that military success is not sufficient to win. I am here to make the case for strengthening our capacity to use soft power and for better integrating it with hard power. What is clear to me is that there is a need for a dramatic increase in spending on the civilian instruments of national security—diplomacy, strategic communications, foreign assistance, civic action, and economic reconstruction and development.[79]

A year later, in an address before students at the National Defense University (NDU) and prior to the 2008 presidential election, Secretary Gates reaffirmed the need to integrate hard and soft power tools into a "balanced strategy," stating:

> This morning, I want to discuss the span of threats our country faces, assess the military capabilities we need ... Lest there be any doubt, this is a speech about hard power ... Over the long term, we cannot kill or capture our way to victory. Nonmilitary efforts—these tools of persuasion and inspiration—were indispensable to the outcome of the defining ideological struggle of the 20th century. They are just as indispensable in the 21st century—and perhaps even more so.[80]

An earlier effort to combine military and nonmilitary programs in troubled areas occurred during President John F. Kennedy's administration. Confronted with the challenge of Soviet proxy wars, Marxist insurgencies, and guerrilla warfare in Latin America, the Army Special Forces were rebuilt and authorized to wear the Green Beret as a mark of distinction.[81] Kennedy's "Alliance for Progress" with Latin American countries lasted from 1961 to 1969 and was the equivalent of a Marshall Plan to work in combination with a "peace corps of talented men and women" who would dedicate themselves to the progress and peace of developing countries by engaging in economic and social development work.[82] In recent years, the U.S. Naval Forces Southern Command and U.S. 4th Fleet, which includes elements of the 26th Marine Expeditionary Unit out of Camp Lejeune, North Carolina, has executed "Operation Continuing Promise."[83] These are programs of humanitarian and civic assistance to provide access to quality health, dental, and veterinary care at no cost while sharing healthcare knowledge and best practices with local healthcare providers in eight Caribbean and Latin American countries. At one time, of course, these operations would have been an expression of American goodwill and friendship, but today they are treated as an exercise of soft power.

International Use of Soft Power

The United States is not the only major country that has turned to soft power approaches, for which they are used by other democratic and non-democratic systems alike. The European Union (EU), for instance, in preparation for its enlargement reformed a number of important policies in 1999 and adopted a soft power-based "Agenda 2000." Existing Western European members were reassured by the message that there would be a "more influential European voice in world affairs, a broader, and therefore more effective, cooperation in dealing with challenges," while the attraction to new members from Central, Eastern, and Southeastern Europe would derive from "democratic and social stability … enhanced prosperity … a return to European political and cultural traditions that were denied them for decades."[84] The EU's commitment to nonmilitary instrumentalities has also led to significant reductions in their military budgets and to the charge that "America seems to be hard power incarnate and Europe the embodiment of soft power."[85]

Qatar

The tiny emirate of Qatar is a contemporary example of a very small country achieving disproportionate influence by virtue of a clever, active foreign policy that leverages its nonmilitary assets. Thus the Fédération Internationale de Football Association, the governing body for world soccer, awarded Qatar the right to host the World Cup Finals in 2022. Qatar beat the bids from Japan, Australia, South Korea, and the United States. The country has an indigenous population of about 300,000—with an additional 1.1 million inhabitants who are mostly contract workers—and the highest GDP per capita in the world. Qatar markets itself as a cosmopolitan, world-class water sports tourist destination, with sandy beaches, sitting out on a peninsula surrounded by the Arabian Gulf.[86] Led by Emir Hamad bin Khalifa al-Thani, Qatar has gained a seat at the power table by creating the brand "Qatar" emphasizing "niche diplomacy" or "the concentration of resources in specific areas best able to generate significant returns."[87] Qatar's niche is conflict mediation; however, its trump card is not its oil reserves, but rather Al Jazeera, the Doha-based first Arab satellite news channel founded in 1996. Al Jazeera is mostly funded by the Qatari government, just as the BBC is funded by the British government. Though some argue that Al Jazeera operates as "one organization, two messages"[88] with one message for the Arab world and another for the West, its influence among the peoples of the region has provided Qatar with enough bona fides to host the conference that led to the Doha Agreements among the rival Lebanese factions on 21 May 2008.[89] In pursuit of its ambitious foreign policy, Qatar supported the Arab Spring and participated in the United Nations (UN) supported humanitarian intervention in Libya by sending four French-made Mirage fighter jets to help maintain a no-fly zone.[90]

The People's Republic of China

In the PRC, almost a month before Secretary Gates's 2007 Landon Lecture, President Hu Jintao called for enhancing Chinese culture as part of the soft power of the country, in a speech to the 17th National Congress of the Communist Party of China.[91] Since then, the PRC has proactively revved up its "charm campaign," as exemplified by a great display of modern weaponry at the 2009 National Day Ceremony to commemorate the 60th anniversary of the founding of the PRC, and the use of futuristic settings, 3D and 4D films at the 2010 Shanghai World Expo. Strategic communication (e.g. public affairs, information operations, and psychological operations), foreign assistance, and cultural tools are being integrated into its foreign policy.[92] In addition to the now familiar nationalistic Chinese martial arts films and performing arts troupes like Shen Yun, about 400 hundred Confucian Institutes that teach Chinese language and culture have sprouted in 80 countries all over the world including in Africa and the United States.[93] Eric Teo Chu Cheow of the Singapore Institute of International Affairs reports that "in Southeast Asia, Chinese culture, cuisine, calligraphy, cinema, curios, art, acupuncture, herbal medicine, and fashion fads have all emerged in regional culture."[94] In Africa, in addition to the ubiquitous Confucian Institutes, the Chinese have focused on development programs, trade, and energy. Chinese support of natural resource-rich countries with repressive regimes presents a major challenge to Western hopes for prosperous African democracies, committed to free trade, human rights, and the rule of law.[95]

In Latin America, where the United States has exercised hegemonic influence for centuries, in addition to seeking access to markets and natural resources, the PRC seeks to gradually erode American influence and has made inroads by stressing nonthreatening cultural and educational programs.

According to NDU professor Evan Ellis, the sources of U.S. influence are "the affinity of the world's youth for American music, media, and lifestyle, the widespread use of the English language in business and technology, or the number of elites who have learned their professions in U.S. institutions."[96] The core of Chinese soft power in the Latin American region is "the widespread perception that the PRC ... will present tremendous business opportunities in the future and will be a power to be reckoned with globally." He then identifies seven component parts of this perception ranging from hopes for future access to Chinese markets to China as the "wave of the future."[97] A number of limitations exist to Chinese soft power in Latin America, however, such as cultural gaps in consumer preferences and attitudes toward authority in business dealings.

> ... the sources of U.S. influence are "the affinity of the world's youth for American music, media, and lifestyle, the widespread use of the English language in business and technology, or the number of elites who have learned their professions in U.S. institutions."

Language is another powerful barrier to closer ties as well as Chinese lack of knowledge regarding Latin America, stigmatization of military officers who participate in military exchanges with China, and the competition created by increased interaction with India, Russia, and Iran. In particular, Ellis highlights that Chinese failure to fully integrate into local communities creates a "not one of us" attitude that translates into mistrust.[98]

In order to assuage growing concerns about China's military intentions and economic policies, the PRC has more recently launched a new public relations campaign seeking to improve its image abroad. The overall plan is to eliminate the perception that China presents a threat to the United States. It includes a 17-minute promotion film shown in Chinese consulates and embassies around the world, as well as a one-minute promotional video shown on six giant screens from 17 January to 14 February 2011 in New York's Times Square for 22 hours a day. The video emphasized life in Beijing and Shanghai featuring attractive urban Chinese people on the screen as well as known celebrities such as basketball player Yao Ming, piano virtuoso Lang Lang, and astronaut Yang Liwei. To measure the video's audience impact, Chinese television staffers interviewed passersby and asked four China experts, including Stanford University's Thomas Fingar, former chairman of the National Intelligence Council, to provide on-camera commentary and feedback.[99]

Chinese government-led efforts at foreign communications, in order to promote a better image to the outside world, have met with limited results, however, largely because the West enjoys more discursive power and due to the lack of free expression in Chinese civil society.[100] Another reason behind the growing distrust of Chinese intentions is the lack of transparency about its growing military capabilities and increasingly aggressive behavior. For example, in early March 2011, soon after its U.S. media campaign, China announced an increase of 13 percent in its FY 2011 defense budget, a projected rise faster than the previous year's 7.5 percent increase. Since the announced budget excluded special programs such as a new stealth fighter and at least one aircraft carrier, experts estimated that the actual defense spending is much higher. Additionally, in the same month, China engaged in confrontations with Japan, South Korea, and the Philippines in disputed territories in the East and South China Seas.[101]

Cuba

The effective use of command and co-optation strategies in a small nation-state is best illustrated by the 50-plus years of dictatorship by the aging brothers Fidel and Raul Castro. Cuba, a small country of 11 million people located 90 miles from Key West, Florida, has been a challenge to the U.S. for five decades. The survival of the Castro brothers' regime is owed not only to the repressive system set up with the help of the East German secret police (Stasi), but also to their effective statecraft.[102] In the early years of the Cuban Revolution, the Castros and Che Guevara tried to export their guerrilla warfare model, or "foco" theory, to the Third World to create more insurgencies. The Castro brothers' regime remains in the Department of State's (DOS) state supporters of terrorism since over the decades they have advised, helped, trained, supported, and financed guerrilla groups and terrorists ranging from the Irish Revolutionary Army, Carlos the Jackal, Uruguayan Tupamaros, Tupac Amarus Revolutionary Movement in Peru, to the Fuerzas Armadas Revolucionarias de Colombia.[103] In the past, the Cuban leaders worked with anti-U.S. regimes (e.g. Chile under Salvador Allende, Sandinistas' Nicaragua, Gaddafi's Libya, Saddam's Iraq, Khomeini's Iran) and continues to work closely with anti-American leaders like Venezuela's Hugo Chavez and Bolivia's Evo Morales, U.S. rivals Russia and China (to be consistent with Russia), and U.S. enemies North Korea and Iran.[104]

During the Cold War, Cuba was a Soviet ally sending troops in the 1970s and 1980s to fight proxy wars in Third World locales such as Angola, Mozambique, and Guinea-Bisseau. About 1,500 Cuban troops including tank and helicopter crews also engaged in combat operations against the Israel Defense Forces in the 1973 Yom Kippur War.[105] During the 1980s, Cuban military contingents were operating in 16 countries.[106] The long-term survival can also be traced to a combination of strategic alliances with the Soviet Union, leftist elements in Europe and Latin America, as well as successful disinformation, espionage, and media manipulation campaigns.[107]

Over the decades, in addition to deploying military forces on three continents, the Castro brothers have presided over a series of propaganda (soft power) campaigns for foreign consumption. They have ranged from Fidel's 16 October 1953 "History Will Absolve Me" speech to the legendary 1956 landing of the ship "Granma" carrying the group that initiated the Cuban Revolution and the co-opting of an independent, third-party messenger, New York Times reporter Herbert Matthews, who brought international fame to Castro's guerrillas. Cuba also produced and disseminated internationally acclaimed films such as Memorias del Subdesarrollo (Memories of Underdevelopment, 1968), Lucia (1969) and Fresa y Chocolate (Strawberry and Chocolate, 1993); and promoted the personality cult of Che Guevara and the "heroic guerrilla" mythology.[108]

Perhaps the most successful Cuban initiative has been its so-called medical diplomacy campaign. The regime has derived "symbolic capital" (i.e. goodwill, influence, and prestige) well beyond what would have been possible for any small country, and this has helped to maintain Cuba as a player on the world stage. In recent years, medical diplomacy has been instrumental in providing "material capital" as Cuba has negotiated oil deals with Venezuela or obtained aid, credit, and trade agreements in exchange for doctors. This has helped keep the revolution afloat during economic trying times. Under this outreach and penetration program, approximately 37,000 Cuban doctors and medical personnel have been sent to 87 countries.

The program also includes giving free medical treatment to low-income Latin Americans and providing free medical training to disadvantaged students from around the globe. What began as the implementation of a core value of the revolution, namely health as a basic human right for all peoples, has continued as both an "idealistic and a pragmatic pursuit."[109]

Attracting tourists to world-class beachfront hotels unaffordable to the average Cuban and cooperating with international filmmakers in works like the 2004 Guevara biopic *The Motorcycle Diaries* serve to project the country's image as a travel destination.[110] Cuban music like the cha-cha, mambo, and salsa, the vaunted Buena Vista Social Club, and other popular cultural exports like the renowned Cuban ballet and dance troupes travel the world to make friends and influence people.[111] Despite the travel ban, American students led by sympathizing academics are invited under academic and cultural exchange programs used by the regime to show the benefits and progressiveness of the Cuban Communist system. Perhaps the best example of Castro's successful command of nonmilitary soft power instrumentalities to deal with its opponents was its masterful media manipulation of the Elian Gonzalez case in 2000, an event that significantly diminished the power and influence of the anti-Castro Cuban-American lobby, covered up the failings of the Cuban dictatorship, exploited U.S. immigration policies, and enhanced Castro's image as a defiant anti-American icon.[112]

Application of Soft Power Approaches

Since Nye coined the soft power terminology, it has generated vast literature and led to U.S. policies and strategies that have been utilized, for instance, in the Iraq War, the War on Terror, and in Eastern Europe during the transition from Communism.[113] In his first major foreign policy address in Cairo 4 June 2009, President Obama reached out to the Muslim world with a commitment to use soft, persuasive approaches:

I also believe that events in Iraq have reminded America of the
need to use diplomacy and build international consensus to resolve
our problems whenever possible. Indeed, we can recall the words
of Thomas Jefferson, who said: 'I hope that our wisdom will grow
with our power, and teach us that the less we use our power the
greater it will be.[114]

Nye's soft-power concept has become a standard, despite the fact that there is
no empirical data or theory to support its claims. Kroenig et.al. ("Kroenig"
study)[115] hypothesizes that to apply soft power effectively a state must do three
things: communicate to an intended target in a functioning marketplace
of ideas, persuade the target to change its attitude on a relevant political
issue, and ensure that the target's newly held attitude influences international
political outcomes. The three preconditions for effective soft power use are
necessary but not sufficient for a state to effectively employ soft power. Their
argument also underscored the critical fact that states do not control some
key resources, like national culture, needed to employ soft power. Their study
examined the existence of these conditions when soft power was utilized
by the U.S. in the Iraq War, the War on Terror, and democracy promotion
experiences. They found that soft power strategies failed in Iraq and the War
on Terror because the conditions were absent but led to success in democracy
promotion in the post-communist transitions in Eastern Europe.[116]

In Iraq, for instance, the initial counterterrorism (CT) approach, albeit
consistent with the U.S. Army Training and Doctrine Command (TRADOC)
on low-intensity conflict, focused mostly on kinetic (violent) engagements
with terrorists and insurgents.[117] The CT approach gave way in 2006 to a
COIN strategy consistent with the updated *Army Field Manual No. 3-24*
that follows a population-centric approach to win "hearts and minds."[118]
The goal was to peel away or insulate the people in order to drain support
for the insurgency and "the goal ... went well beyond mere rhetoric" as
concrete steps were taken such as: monetary payments in compensation for
property damage during raids, post-conflict reconstruction, information
campaigns to include paying to plant favorable articles in Iraqi papers, pre-
deployment training in mock Iraqi villages in the California desert, and a
military "surge" to provide more civilian protection and security. Kroenig
argues that all of these efforts failed because some of the preconditions for
success were absent.[119]

A set of damaging events interfered with the long-term efforts by the United States to win hearts and minds in Iraq. One of them was the failure to properly handle the anarchy and looting that occurred, particularly in Baghdad, in the early days of the occupation. At best, it reflected an American lack of adequate post-war contingency planning and, at worst, lack of understanding about the sectarian and cultural differences. Secondly, the torture scandal at Abu Ghraib prison revealed in 2004 betrayed the content of the message we were trying to send with the change in regime (i.e. respect for and protection of individual liberties and human rights) and significantly weakened American moral authority. Who can forget the iconic image of the hooded prisoner with outstretched arms attached to wires while standing on a box?[120] Despite former Secretary of Defense Donald Rumsfeld's claim that the abuses were the acts of rogue soldiers and not approved policy, the torture scandal did irreparable damage to the U.S. global image. To his credit, after the revelations became public, Secretary Rumsfeld submitted his resignation to President Bush, who declined to accept it.[121] Third, the idea of forcefully exporting democracy to the Middle East runs counter to the accumulating evidence that it breeds ethnic hatred and instability.[122] Finally, and perhaps most important, there was the "deep contradiction between the democracy the United States said it was trying to build and the methods it employed to battle the insurgency."[123]

The Kroenig study provides a useful set of criteria to determine which types of problems are most amenable to soft power strategies since they only succeed under fairly restrictive conditions. First, the soci-

...the idea of forcefully exporting democracy to the Middle East runs counter to the accumulating evidence that it breeds ethnic hatred and instability.

ety must be considered. It should have a functioning marketplace of ideas and be receptive to communication and persuasion. Strategic communication has been defined as the "orchestration and/or synchronization of actions, images, and words to achieve a desired effect."[124]

Next, the target audience in the society should be capable of influencing international outcomes in a manner favorable to U.S. interests. Third, to succeed, the U.S. should "shape the battlefield" by, for instance, advocating for an open media and a reduction of censorship. Finally, the campaign should be waged indirectly through intermediaries trusted by the target audience.

That is, independent, third party sources with no U.S. ties or interests need to be identified to act as messengers.[125] Regarding the endorsement of soft power by U.S. policymakers (e.g. Secretary Clinton and Secretary Gates), the Kroenig study warns that when it comes to soft power, "the U.S. foreign policy elite is at risk of exaggerating the effectiveness of soft power (rather than under-utilizing it) as a tool of foreign policy."[126] In addition, "Analysts who suggest that soft power can easily be substituted for hard power or who maintain that soft power should provide an overarching guide to the formulation of U.S. foreign policy are badly mistaken. It is not helpful to effective policy making to use the phrase 'soft power' as a way of arguing against the use of military force."[127]

Smart Power

In 2004, former Deputy Assistant Secretary of State Suzanne Nossel introduced the phrase "smart use of power" to promote U.S. interests through a stable grid of allies, institutions, and norms.[128] According to Nossel, in the 2002 National Security Strategy the Bush administration pledged not only to fight terrorism and "pre-empt" threats, but also to "actively work to bring the hope of democracy, development, free markets, and free trade to every corner of the world." But all of these were traditional liberal internationalist themes.[129] Progressives were therefore encouraged to "take back the fight" by reframing U.S. foreign policy according to their "abiding belief than an ambitious agenda to advance freedom, trade, and human rights is the best long-term guarantee of the United States' security."[130]

For Nossel, a "renewed liberal internationalist strategy recognizes that military power and humanitarian endeavors can be mutually reinforcing" if one turns Bush's preemption policy around by recasting traditional liberal priorities like counter-proliferation and economic development as preemptors of threats that would preclude the need for military action.[131] Several recommendations were: a new military branch composed of a standing force dedicated exclusively to postwar stabilization and reconstruction; burden sharing with allies; and reformation of the UN's bureaucracy, field capabilities, anti-Western membership blocs, redundant committees, and U.S. diplomatic approach.[132] In sum, the "smart use of power" originally referred to a reframing of foreign policies away from the neoconservative reliance on the use of force to fight terrorism and democratize regimes.

Joseph P. Nye Jr. has claimed that smart power "is a term I developed in 2003 to counter the misperception that soft power alone can produce effective foreign policy … Thus the need for smart strategies that combine the tools of both hard and soft power."[133] The original conceptualization, however, emphasized soft power as a standalone policy approach, while Nossel's referred to a synthesis of soft and hard power tools that reinforces both.[134] Despite the paternity dispute, members of academia, the think tanks, and government officials soon began to bandwagon behind the concept of smart power. In particular, those who feared appearing weak on national security and felt uncomfortable with the "soft" aspect of Nye's power terminology welcomed the new approach—"Most progressives approve of the concept, but hate the name—'soft power' just sounds so … weak."[135]

Thus, in 2006 the Center for Strategic and International Studies (CSIS) declared that "America's image and influence are in decline around the world. To maintain a leading role in global affairs, the United States must move from eliciting fear and anger to inspiring optimism and hope."[136] To attain that goal the CSIS launched a bipartisan Commission on Smart Power led by Nye and Richard L. Armitage as co-chairs to "develop a vision to guide America's global engagement."[137] The commission's final report sought to integrate hard and soft power into a hybrid "smart power" and recommended a smart power strategy that included: rebuilding and reinvigorating the foundation of alliances, partnerships, and institutions that serve our interests; elevating the role of development in U.S. foreign policy and developing a more unified approach to global development beginning with public health; public diplomacy directed at building people-to-people relationships, particularly with youth; economic integration and expansion of free trade; and addressing climate change and energy insecurity through technology and innovation.[138] To implement the strategy, it called for a strategic reassessment of how the U.S. Government (USG) is organized, coordinated, and budgeted in order to organize for success.[139]

That set of goals reprised Nossel's argument and is consistent with those advocated by proponents of a "new global agenda" that seeks to tackle poverty, bridge divides, and build institutions for the 21st century. The causal chain being promulgated is that "Poverty, disease, and malnutrition cause civil strife, degradation, and conflict, which spills over borders, imperiling national and international security." The research, issues, and policy initiatives at the top of this global agenda include a list of items ranging from reducing nuclear armaments and stemming proliferation to fostering inclusion of new economic powers.[140]

As noted earlier, Secretary Gates in his Langdon Lecture (2007) and NDU speech (2008) had introduced hard and soft power language not only to distinguish between defense and civilian missions, but also to call for their better integration.[141] However, it was not until the 2009 Senate confirmation hearing of Senator Hillary Clinton as nominee for Secretary of State that the new concept of "smart power" catapulted into the headlines. At the hearing, Senator Clinton touted it four times in her opening statement and nine times during her testimony by saying, "I believe that American leadership has been wanting, but is still wanted. We must use what has been called 'smart power,' the full range of tools at our disposal, which include diplomatic, economic, military, political and cultural tools ... With smart power, diplomacy will be the vanguard of foreign policy."[142]

The State Department's First Quadrennial Diplomacy and Development Review (QDDR) in turn seeks to blend soft power tools of diplomacy and development with the new global agenda by "embracing 21st century state-craft to connect the private and civic sectors with our foreign policy work ... by better using connection technologies and expanding, facilitating, and streamlining our public-private partnership process."[143] The DOS is fully committed to smart power and has made "digital democracy," the application of new social media to shape global political action, a cornerstone of U.S. diplomacy.

Military force may sometimes be necessary to protect our people and our interests. But diplomacy and development will be equally important in creating conditions for a peaceful, stable, and prosperous world. That is the essence of smart power—using all the tools at our disposal.[144] Predictably, advocacy groups and defense contractors soon jumped into the smart power bandwagon. The Mitre Corporation, for instance, soon followed up with their own "Corporate Initiative in Smart Power" seeking to employ an effective blend of coercive, hard power (defensive/offensive boots on the ground) as well as persuasive soft power (diplomacy, development).[145] A certain amount of confusion has resulted, however, from the failure to distinguish between the tools of power and the use of power. For if "using all the tools at our disposal" is the essence of smart power, then the unanswered question is what criteria is utilized to prioritize goals and means? Using all the tools at our disposal requires a process of identification, evaluation, and selection between coercive and persuasive tools. Secretary Gates, as described above, was concerned with the integration and balancing of hard and soft power tools. The critical issue is how is that integration and balancing to be done, by whom, and on what terms? The obvious answer is that the proper balancing depends on the strategic goals that are being

> *A certain amount of confusion has resulted, however, from the failure to distinguish between the tools of power and the use of power.*

sought, and the final choice between the use of military or nonmilitary tools rests with the president as chief executive and commander in chief.

The Arab Spring and Smart/Soft Power

Smart power should mean just the opposite of the non-smart use of power. The non-smart use of power is the ineffective or inappropriate use of the instruments of power in a particular context. It is choosing carrots when sticks would do the job and vice versa. The smart use of power is neither a new type of power nor a power attribute, but rather a better way of using power capabilities—both military and nonmilitary. That is to say, it is the exercise of good statecraft; statecraft seeks the optimal use of power in the most effective way to carry out strategic plans in order to achieve strategic goals. It is a how—an intellectual activity involving knowledge, experience, and judgment—by a who. The who ultimately are those with the status, authority, qualities, and attributes of leadership. When statesmen exercise their best judgment by setting and prioritizing strategic goals, creatively and effectively choosing the proper means of implementation, and selecting the best tools available in the toolbox, then power is being used in a smart way. Does that mean that the desired or predicted outcomes will follow? Not necessarily, since there is always an element of risk.

The chaotic Arab Spring was driven both by demographics and politics. Approximately 60 percent of the Arab population is under age 30 with a median age of 26.[146] This youth bulge has "both the fastest-rising levels of schooling and the highest level of youth unemployment in the world" and lacks the quality of life and opportunities that television and the new media portray elsewhere.[147] The combination of a life of privation and rising expectations is an explosive mix when combined with inability to express the accumulated frustration. The Mukhabarat state, called a "police state" in the West, under which most young Arabs have lived, denied them the political space to negotiate their demands. Egypt, as the cultural, geographic, and demographic center of the Arab world, presented to them an example of what is possible. The popular overthrow of Mubarak occurred with less than 1,000 casualties. A successful Egyptian transition to a representative system where repressed secular parties can organize and operate would be a blow to al-Qaeda's terrorist narrative. As a counterpoint, the upheaval in Libya shows how to attain reform through violent action.

Egypt

The "Arab Spring" unrest, first in Tunisia and later in Egypt, Libya, Yemen, Bahrain, Syria, and other countries in the region presents a serious threat to regional stability and longstanding American economic and security interests. In addition to the ever-present issue of oil resources, there are also military basing and cooperative arrangements that are at stake. The protest movements were largely organized by groups and individuals through American produced instrumentalities like the Internet and social media sites like Facebook and Twitter. On 27 January 2011, the Mubarak regime, in order to prevent the spread of anti-Mubarak messages and to cripple mass organizing efforts, shut down the Internet and cell phone service. By ordering the big four Egyptian service providers—Link Egypt, Vodafone/Raya, Telecom Egypt, and Etisalat Misr—to shut down all international connections to the Internet, the government in effect threw a switch that caused a 90 percent drop in data traffic.[148] Government cutoffs of information flows have previously taken place in Nepal (2005) and Myanmar (2007); in 40 other countries, particularly in China and Cuba, filtering of Internet services and sites is an established practice. What was surprising to many, however, was the scope and scale of the 2011 Egyptian shutdown.[149]

Secretary Gates and Secretary Clinton both had understood Mubarak's actions as an attempt to maintain control, and the message they clearly sent to the Mubarak regime was that no American weapons and ammunition should be used against the peaceful protesters. At the same time, President Obama, after talking to Mubarak in private, publicly asked him "to reverse the actions that they've taken to interfere with access to the Internet, to cell phone service, and to social networks that do so much to connect people in the 21st century." By doing so, he was in effect tying the hands of staunch ally Mubarak. President Obama was criticized for ignoring the law of unintended consequences and assuming that the subsequent series of geopolitical outcomes—i.e. the eventual ousting of Mubarak and spreading unrest to other friendly countries in the Middle East and North Africa—would advance U.S. national interests.[150]

Concerns emerged within both the DOD and DOS as the unrest spilled over into another critical ally, the Kingdom of Bahrain, headquarters of the U.S. Navy's 5th Fleet. The strategic value of Bahrain to the United States and the West is very significant as the 5th Fleet supports our efforts in Iraq and Afghanistan and is a deterrent against a nuclear Iran. As a kingdom ruled by Sunni Muslims where the majority of the population is Shiite, the possible collapse of the pro-American monarchy raised the specter of a pro-Iranian, anti-American Shiite takeover under the guise of democratization. In the short term, the important question was how would the Obama administration react if the Bahrain government resorted to force? In Bahrain, the United States has less comparative leverage than its adjacent neighbor Saudi Arabia that favored strong action against the Shiites in Bahrain. Would the U.S. choose the democratic values against the national interest road by siding with the Shiite opposition against its Sunni allies? What was the regional strategy being followed by the USG? As government and opposition groups clashed in Manama, the capital of Bahrain, the UN High Commissioner for Human Rights, the EU, and Human Rights Watch criticized and urged the Bahrain government to stop its security forces from using force.[151]

Statecraft is constrained by institutional and individual factors. In the early days of the 2011 Egyptian "Lotus Revolution," the basic analytic assumption in the U.S. intelligence community was that the Mubarak regime was stable.[152] For three decades, the United States has had excellent military-to-military relations with Egypt providing it with $1.5 billion in annual military assistance, a hard power tool. Egyptian military leaders participated in the U.S. International Military Education and Training Program (IMET), one of whose purposes is to train an ethical military. The IMET program under the U.S. Defense Security Cooperation Agency of DOD is a security assistance program that provides training on a grant basis to students from allied and friendly nations. Funding is appropriated from the International Affairs budget of the DOS. Overall objectives of the IMET program are: to further the goal of regional stability through effective, mutually beneficial military-to-military relations which culminate in increased understanding and defense cooperation between the United States and foreign countries; and to increase the ability of foreign national military and civilian personnel to absorb and maintain basic democratic values and protect internationally recognized human rights.

Just like the failure to foresee the Soviet collapse, the revolt in Egypt appeared to be a foreseeable event. The North African and Middle Eastern Arab countries in revolt were led by aging authoritarians entering a period of political succession. In Tunisia, the immolation of a despaired food peddler acted as the catalyst for suppressed anger and disaffection with the regime. Instability was particularly foreseeable in Egypt; to polarize the political system along the lines of his secular government party versus the Islamic Muslim Brotherhood, Mubarak prevented secular opposition parties from organizing and operating freely for decades. It was also known that Mubarak planned to install his unpopular son Gamal as his replacement; and that the country had an uneducated, unemployed, impoverished, and restless youth bulge. These systemic problems signaled that trouble lay ahead despite the image of stability portrayed by the repressive apparatus. Neither the timing nor the magnitude of the eruption was knowable, of course, but a disruptive course of events was predictable and appropriate probabilistic scenarios and war gaming exercises should have been conducted well in advance.[153]

It is reasonable to assume that within the U.S. military and diplomatic community there was support for the undemocratic Mubarak regime. He was, after all, a staunch ally, a bulwark against Iran, and a key player in our war efforts in Iraq and Afghanistan. At the beginning of the crisis, a number of geostrategic reasons could be adduced in favor of a U.S. presidential statement supporting the regime and just asking it to exercise restraint. If confronted, the administration could have justified its stance by raising a host of reasons ranging from a national security interest in preventing a repetition of the 1979 Iranian Revolution to maintaining access to a vital chokepoint, the Suez Canal; from sustaining the Egyptian-Israeli peace treaty to preventing contagion to other countries and avoiding another intervention in the Arab world. The initial tilt toward Mubarak based on faulty or absent intelligence was reflected in Secretary of State Clinton's public statement on 25 January 2011, that "our assessment is that the Egyptian Government is stable and is looking for ways to respond to the legitimate needs and interests of the Egyptian people."[154]

As millions of Egyptians took to the streets in Cairo, Suez, Alexandria, and other cities, however, democracy promoters insisted that the United States be "on the right side of history." It would require supporting popular democratic movements; confirming the role played by the "new media" (e.g. Internet, Twitter, YouTube, Facebook, and cell phones) in informing and mobilizing the population; affirming a moral duty to oust a recalcitrant dictator; and setting an example of peaceful regime change for the youthful and restive Arab "street." After all, it was added, this is what American policymakers had sought when they promoted democratic change. Was the Obama administration pursuing a freedom agenda through soft power means? Obviously, both sides had powerful arguments in support of their respective positions. It is also apparent that at some point, as events unfolded, the administration could not continue its middle-of-the-road strategy; it could not support Mubarak or tolerate a "Tiananmen Square" type of crackdown while at the same time supporting the pro-democracy demonstrations.[155]

A choice had to be made either to pressure the Mubarak regime to exercise "restraint" in the use of force, or to "refrain" from using force to save itself, or to give up power altogether. The administration appeared to adopt a position in support of an "orderly transition" from Mubarak to a new regime since the risk calculus had to consider as possible outcomes a significant loss of lives, loss or damage to important United States strategic interests, or both. Whether Mubarak would have resorted to ruthless violence, as Muammar Gaddafi subsequently did in Libya and Bashar al-Assad in Syria, had the U.S. acquiesced to it, is counterfactual. But after 30 years of deep ties with Mubarak's military, the U.S. had sufficient knowledge of the Egyptian Army to consider it as a professional institution committed to the country that would not fire on the people.

The lack of a representative organized opposition party or group to negotiate with the Egyptian government, except for the Muslim Brotherhood and other Islamists, complicated the situation and raised the ante for those who favored a quick ousting of Mubarak. In the end, lacking a grand strategy and actionable intelligence to prioritize and guide a course of action, the administration struggled through this initial phase of the revolutionary process. The administration placed some hope that Mohammed El Baradei, the Nobel laureate and former head of the UN nuclear watchdog agency, the International Atomic Energy Agency, would be able to attract enough support. The floundering performance suggested that a regional strategy was lacking as the opposition proactively used soft power tools while the U.S. administration was reacting to events.[156] The instability of the Mubarak regime led to a readjustment of U.S. policy, the fall of Mubarak on 11 February, and to a greater appreciation of the role played by the new soft power tools in the Middle East and North Africa. The lesson learned

> The lesson learned is that new technologies offer new means to exercise influence...

is that new technologies offer new means to exercise influence, and that they are increasingly being used by popular movements in order to sway large portions of the population and challenge existing regimes.

Libya

On 15 February 2011, a few days after the fall of Mubarak, popular unrest broke out in Libya, Africa's third largest oil producer. Long-standing dictator Muammar Abu Minyar al-Gaddafi reacted by brutally cracking down on the civilian demonstrators. UN Secretary General Ban Ki-moon accused Libya of "firing on civilians from warplanes and helicopters" and killing thousands of protesters as paramilitary goons were set loose on the streets of Benghazi, the cradle of the revolt, and Tripoli.[157] Vowing to die as a martyr, Gaddafi ignored the international community's call for restraint. In disgust, high Libyan officials like the ambassadors to the United States, the UN, Malaysia, Australia, Indonesia, the Arab League, and India, resigned their posts, and the Interior Minister Abdel Fattah Younes al Abidi defected to the rebels. As Eastern Libya fell under rebel soldiers' control, the dictator was accused of recruiting African mercenaries to put down the revolt. From Qatar, Muslim Sunni cleric Yusuf al-Qaradawi, the spiritual leader of the Muslim Brotherhood, issued a fatwa asking Libyan soldiers not to shoot people but to kill Gaddafi.[158] Meanwhile, U.S. policymakers struggled to find some leverage over the Libyan dictator. Gaddafi had been a rabid anti-American who provided terrorists with training camps and had to be bombed in 1986 by Ronald Reagan.[159] Until 2003, Libya was on the DOS list of state sponsors of terrorism. After the 9/11 attacks and following Operation Iraqi Freedom, it was rumored that Gaddafi feared that he would be the next one facing an American intervention since Libya was close to developing a nuclear weapon. Libya had moved to achieve a rapprochement with the West since 1999 by accepting responsibility for the Lockerbie bombing and paying $10 million in compensation.[160] President George W. Bush working with British Prime Minister Tony Blair sought to reintegrate Libya into the international community by lifting UN sanctions and obtaining a UN resolution demanding that Libya give up its weapons of mass destruction (WMD) program. Gaddafi complied by giving up Libya's nuclear and chemical weapons programs and in exchange the DOS took Libya off its terrorist list. Unlike Egypt, however, the Libyan government only received a meager U.S. $1 million a year for the country's disarmament program, and military-to-military ties were minimal. When the 2011 revolt began, U.S. leverage over the Libyan situation was practically nil. As a major exporter of high quality oil to Europe, and significant investor in countries like Italy, Libya also had a protective cushion against international economic sanctions. Yet, as noted below, Gaddafi's ruthless approach to the uprising eventually led the U.S. and its NATO allies to act.

Secretary Clinton had sought to maximize the potential of new media technology in the development and practice of the civilian side of our foreign policy. In a foreign policy address to the Council on Foreign Relations on 15 July 2009, she said, "We are working at the State Department to ensure that our government is using the most innovative technologies not only to speak and listen ... but to widen opportunities for those who are too often left on the margins."[161] Secretary Clinton brought along young entrepreneurs like Alec Ross, Senior Advisor for Innovation to the DOS, to launch the new technology-driven "21st century statecraft."[162] In early 2010, she announced the DOS "Internet Freedom" initiative, promising to make online freedoms part of the State Department's 21st century statecraft. The Internet, she suggested, could be a powerful force in support of political freedom, and the United States "must put these tools in the hands of people around the world who will use them to advance democracy and human rights ... "[163] The difference between the 21st century statecraft and conventional diplomacy, she continued, was, "one of the things that we recognized since early in the Obama administration is that leveraging our digital networks, we can now engage government-to-people, people-to-people, and people-to-government."[164]

A year later, in the midst of the revolutions in Egypt and Libya, the leaders of both countries responded to the freedom initiative by shutting down the Internet. Soon thereafter, in a second speech on Internet freedom at George Washington University, Secretary Clinton first downplayed its significance: "A debate is currently underway in some circles about whether the Internet is a force for liberation or repression ... I think that debate is largely beside the point."[165]

Following the November 2010 WikiLeaks publication of classified DOS diplomatic cables, she acknowledged that there were limitations and that the Internet should not serve as a weapon of 21st century statecraft:

> The Internet has become the public space of the 21st century – the world's town square, classroom, marketplace, coffeehouse, and nightclub ... These spaces provide an open platform, and so does the Internet. It does not serve any particular agenda, and it never should.[166]

In addition to the need to protect classified information, there were at least two additional concerns: (1) that the new media could be used for political mobilization by atomized or networked individuals very effectively with minimal strategic or actionable foresight on the part of central governments; and (2) that foreign governments now have the capability to control the Internet and through it repress and harm people. At the same time, the Internet continues to be restrained in a myriad of ways. In China, the government censors content and redirects search requests to error pages. In Burma, independent news sites have been taken down with distributed denial of service attacks. In Cuba, the government is trying to create a national intranet, while not allowing citizens to access the global Internet. In Vietnam, bloggers who criticize the government are arrested and abused. In Iran, the authorities block opposition and media websites, target social media, and steal identifying information about their own people in order to hunt them down.[167] Likewise, in Egypt and Libya the authoritarian leaders sought to use the new technologies as weapons of repression.

Something had happened to the "smart power" approach when confronted with a real world situation, for the new media tools were proving to be both a blessing and a curse. Why not turn to conventional diplomacy? While the U.S. had close relations with the Egyptian regime, it lacked direct access to Gaddafi. David Mack, a former senior U.S. diplomat who dealt with Libya, said, "As far as I know, President Obama has never even talked to Colonel Gaddafi."[168] Secretary Clinton tried a televised public appeal to Gaddafi—"Now is the time to stop this unacceptable bloodshed," she said.[169] Gaddafi disagreed with the timing, could not care less about what the U.S.

found unacceptable, and did not stop the bloodshed. President Obama, who had made frequent public statements during the early days of the Mubarak overthrow, did not address the Libyan crisis for eight days. As civilian casualties mounted, Secretary Clinton became the public face of the USG on the Libyan crisis. The president's delay in getting in front of the crisis was first explained as a scheduling conflict and later as a move to give American citizens and diplomatic personnel time to safely depart Libya. But some critics of the president found the explanations disingenuous claiming that the French, German, and British leaders had not only condemned Gaddafi's actions while their citizens were still on Libyan territory, but that the Germans and the British had also sent special forces to retrieve hundreds of citizens from Libya. In his first speech on the Libyan crisis, President Obama said he was considering a "full range of options" and initiating multilateral conversations with European and African countries.[170] The crisis was bringing to the fore the problem of identifying the conditions under which, and to what extent, military power should be employed.

> *The crisis was bringing to the fore the problem of identifying the conditions under which, and to what extent, military power should be employed.*

Then Secretary Clinton again tried conventional diplomacy at the UN Human Rights Council meeting in Geneva by declaring, "It is time for Gaddafi to go—now, without further violence or delay."[171] Gaddafi dismissed the idea of ceding power.[172] Since allowing the crisis to follow its own course was adjudged morally and politically unacceptable, the U.S. and its NATO allies turned to coercive options against Gaddafi and his followers. The options being considered ranged from freezing $30 billion in Gaddafi family assets as well as those of senior Libyan officials, banning weapons sales, asking the Saudis to supply weapons to the opposition, threatening prosecution for crimes against humanity in the International Criminal Court of Justice, to moving ships and aircraft to the Libyan coast, and establishing a no-fly zone over Libyan skies for a multilateral use of force with a coalition composed of European oil consuming countries and the African Union. Openly supporting al-Qaradawi's fatwa was certainly out of the question but was not being discouraged. In other words, the U.S. appeared to be caught in a democratization trap, for no amount of text messaging, Tweeting, e-mailing, cell-phone calling, Facebook interacting, or any other sort of 21st century digital media tool could protect the Libyans from the bullets. Yet that very set of tools had also kept them informed and helped coordinate these revolts and other previous protest movements like those in India (2009), South Korea (2008), and Chile (2006).

Secretary Clinton had originally supported a "no-fly zone" approach to the Libyan crisis but reconsidered following Secretary Gates warnings about it constituting an act of war. But the media soon reported that her position had shifted back after intense internal debate and pressure from National Security Council (NSC) senior directors Samantha Power and Gayle Smith, U.S. ambassador to the UN Susan Rice, and former DOS director of policy planning Dr. Anne-Marie Slaughter.[173] The "ghosts of Rwanda" appeared to haunt this group of former President Clinton officials. Rwanda was a tragedy that President Clinton has referred to as "the biggest regret of his presidency,"[174] but in the Obama administration they were now in a position to overcome those regrets and influence events.

Intense diplomatic negotiations followed with UN Security Council members, the Arab League, and NATO allies, resulting in United Nations Security Council Resolution 1973 (2011), which approved a "no fly zone" over Libya and authorized UN Members under Chapter VII of the UN Chapter to use "all necessary measures" to protect civilians.[175] On 19 March 2011, Operation Odyssey Dawn began against Gaddafi's regime, confirming for some that democracies are more likely to fight wars against non-democracies than amongst themselves.[176] It also marked a difference between Secretary Clinton and Secretary Gates over a strategic policy issue. In his 2009 Foreign Affairs article about a balanced strategy, Secretary Gates had explicitly asserted:

> The United States is the strongest and greatest nation on earth, but there are still limits on what it can do. The power and global reach of its military have been an indispensable contributor to world peace and must remain so. But not every outrage, every act of aggression, or every crisis can or should elicit a U.S. military response.[177]

The disparity in their approaches reflected fundamental differences not only over when to use force but whether the decision should be guided by value-based interests or vital national interests. The core issue is that in any type of political system, whether democratic or non-democratic, "Vital interests are those which a nation deems to be essential, which it will not willingly forsake, and for which if necessary it will fight—diplomatically, politically and militarily."[178] When an interest is vital in nature it trumps lesser ones and leaders are also not willing to compromise.

In the case of Libya, however, President Obama was won over by the case presented by interventionists led by NSC senior aide Samantha Power[179] and supported by Secretary Clinton, Anne-Marie Slaughter, and UN Ambassador Susan Rice, who lined up to push for the use of force to protect civilians as a "humanitarian value-interest." This was in opposition to Secretary Gates, National Security Advisor Thomas E. Donilon, Counterterrorism Chief John O. Brennan, and Director of National Intelligence James Clapper, who seeing no vital interest at stake and concerned about the preservation of national power, had urged caution.[180] While the DOD leadership considered Libya as a non-vital, peripheral interest, the president's decision elevated U.S. credibility in promoting democracy to the status of a vital national interest.[181]

The Larger Meaning of the Arab Spring and Operation Odyssey Dawn

The attributes of great leadership seem to be well-established, namely: vision, integrity, judgment, perseverance, courage, a hunger for innovation, and a willingness to take risks. In the business world, long inhabited by former military, there is one immutable attribute that is shared by great leaders— contextual leadership.[182] Contextual leaders possessed an acute sensitivity to the social, political, technological, and demographic contexts that defined their eras. Lawrence of Arabia considered temperament and judgment as the key to leadership.[183] During the Arab crisis, the middle of the road approach between democracy promotion and resorting to regime change by force sent a mixed message. A critic pointedly asked, "How can the USG make promoting democracy its main priority without even mentioning the idea of vigorously promoting democracy in Iran or Syria or supporting the oppositions in those countries?[184] An almost similar complaint had been raised by Senator Barak Obama in his 2006 book *The Audacity of Hope* when he wrote: "The United States still lacks a coherent national security policy ... Instead of guiding principles, we have what appears to be a series of ad hoc decisions, with dubious results. Why invade Iraq and not North Korea or Burma? Why intervene in Bosnia and not Darfur?"[185]

As noted, the decision to intervene also was intellectually influenced by the Center for a New American Security, where Anne-Marie Slaughter, Gayle

Smith, Susan Rice, and other Obama officials had previously collaborated in a project to prepare a strategic leadership framework, a roadmap for the next president.[186] In the proposal, they recommended that despite the prevalent presumption that America must always be in charge, effective leadership is not always centered in Washington. At times, our interests are best served when others lead with us, or even take our place at the helm.[187]

This was clearly the policy approach adopted by President Obama toward Libya despite DOD's denial that Libya was a vital or major U.S. interest. In the end, the president chose to hedge his bet by moving to enforce a no-fly zone over Libya while refusing to take the lead and committing the U.S. to play a supportive role in what became known as a "coalition of the leaderless."[188] Subsequently, Secretary Gates announced on 23 March that the United Sates would cede command of military operations to NATO and Germany, in disagreement, pulled forces out of the Libyan operation, sending the coalition into temporary disarray. The infighting did not involve the substantive issue of having U.S. troops serving under foreign command since U.S. Admiral James G. Stavridis was the NATO Supreme Allied Commander. The issue was that several European countries also believed that Libya had no relevance to their defense, that it did not involve a vital or major NATO interest.[189]

Michael Vlahos argues that while countries have entered wars to survive, a case can be made that "all of America's wars are wars of choice." As a result, he adds, "American wars must be sold to the public."[190] When making national security decisions of great importance, national leaders must recognize that the United States must act as a superpower by providing leadership, acting from a position of strength with clarity of vision. They must know that we have adversaries and cruel enemies who are searching for vulnerabilities, learning, and adapting their strategies, operations, and tactics as best suits them. On a

American wars must be sold to the public.

global level, the Arab Spring is the battleground of a "world-spanning confrontation" against the international state system. In this confrontation three groups are engaged: the defenders, the seekers, and the enemies of the international system. The defenders are member states in good standing, such as the Gulf States, Israel, and Jordan. The seekers are states like Lebanon, Yemen, Egypt, and Iraq that are moving toward being members in good standing. The enemies are Libya, Syria, other oppressive regimes, and the non-state and anti-state actors like al-Qaeda set against the international state system itself.[191] While the terror attacks of 9/11 triggered a military war of necessity in defense of the nation against al-Qaeda and its Taliban hosts, Operation Odyssey Dawn reflects a more hesitant American entry into the battleground.

Weaponization of the New Media and its Critics

The fusion of the neoconservative freedom agenda with new media "liberation technology" for international political action has been recently examined by political media experts.[192] A participant in the "Internet Freedom" initiative warned about the perils of using Internet freedom as a weapon. Accordingly, the DOS was using an "instrumental" approach that concentrated on preventing states from censoring outside websites, such as Google or YouTube, and only secondarily on private or social uses of digital media. The instrumental approach was criticized for overestimating the value of broadcast media, access to information, and the importance of computers while underestimating the value of media that allows private communications, media tools for local coordination, and the importance of cell phones. Cell phones, in particular, were of great importance as conduits for coordination purposes and as a means of documenting real-time actions through video streaming.[193]

The United States Institute of Peace (USIP) was created by Congress in 1984 to train military and civilian personnel and, according to General Petraeus, to assist in "developing stronger unity of effort between civilian and military elements of government."[194] The USIP reports that in the case of the 2009 Green Movement in Iran, "new media helped to link disparate groups and individuals in the absence of formal organization or effective leadership."[195] One powerful image from the Green Movement, the dissident movement triggered by fraudulent electoral results in Iran, was a video of a young female bystander, Neda Agha-Soltan, being shot dead during a demonstration in Teheran. The incident became a rallying cry as the video went viral on the Internet and was Tweeted around the globe.[196] The Iranian government, however, cracked down on the dissidents by detaining, arresting, and even torturing an undisclosed number.[197] It confirms that governments have become much more sophisticated and effective in using the new media for control and repression. New media as a political weapon in the war of ideas is therefore a double-edged sword and a dangerous one that may be a matter of life and death for political dissidents and activists in authoritarian regimes. In contrast to the instrumental approach, therefore, Shirky proposed an "environmental" view of Internet freedom. Under such interpretation, USG efforts should be directed toward the goal of developing a strong civil society before seeking positive changes, such as pro-democratic regime change, because real world statecraft demands a long-term approach that goes beyond short-term digital tactics.[198]

Two years after the Iranian Green Movement, as the popular uprisings in Tunisia, Egypt, Libya, Yemen, Syria, and other North African and Middle Eastern countries broke out, use of the new media as a soft power weapon appeared to produce both good and bad effects. It was mainly because new media can be "an agent of democracy and peace" or can "just as easily be used to radicalize, exclude and enrage."[199] The new information technologies may provide both capacities and constraints on institutional change within political systems. In effect, government decision makers in developing countries are facing a growing dilemma—they need the new communications technologies in order to accelerate economic development, but these technologies are being used by their opponents to undermine the political structures. Evgeny Morozov, who labeled the new media advocates "Cyber Utopians," convincingly argues that the use of the new media may strengthen rather than weaken repressive regimes. He criticizes adherents of the "Google doctrine," who hold a "fervent conviction that given enough gadgets, connectivity and foreign funding, dictatorships are doomed."[200]

New media experts Shirky and Morozov, who are frequently on the opposite side when it comes to democratization, agree that the U.S. had "not merely done a poor job of establishing digital freedoms elsewhere in the world, but may in fact have damaged that cause."[201] Two reasons are given for that poor performance:

> Washington undermined its claims to leadership when it allowed commercial firms like Amazon and PayPal to cut off payments to WikiLeaks with less due process than is required to get a firm on the terrorist list. The United States was likewise hypocritical when it responded to the recent persecution of Tunisian Internet activists with relative silence, after having so vocally objected to the suppression of free speech in Iran over the past year.[202]

Lack of systematic thinking about the nexus between politics, violence, and new media lay behind the conundrums faced by U.S. policymakers during the Arab Revolution of 2011.[203] The "Internet Freedom" agenda was meant to be a long effort while media democracy activists, drunk on the elixir of instant messaging by Twitter and other media tools, believed that regime change is easy and can be done in a short time. They underestimated the difficult problem of aligning U.S. democratic values of free speech, association, and press with important national interests such as stability, alliance, and partnership maintenance in the Middle East.

Furthermore, the Cyber Utopian emphasis on the power of media tools to affect political change ignored the impact of deeper socioeconomic and political cleavages within Arab societies that influenced the nature and timing of the uprisings. Nikolas Gvosdev points out that in April 2008 a popular movement in support of textile workers began in Egypt using Facebook to attract 70,000 Egyptian Internet users as virtual supporters. However, the group merely engaged in online debates followed by no offline action. In February 2011, the same media tools were given credit for initiating the Mubarak overthrow. So, what had changed in the virtual world that could explain the different outcomes in the real world? According to Gvosdev, nothing had changed in the virtual world, but it was what had happened in the "real world" that mattered. In Egypt, as well as Libya and Yemen, "Aging leaders got older, while stagnant systems remained unchanged, and undesirable succession options loomed."[204]

An information expert asserts that "no democratic transition has occurred solely because of the Internet. But ... no democratic transition can occur today without the Internet."[205] As others have shown, this argument glosses over the increasing ability of governments to shut down Internet access and interfere with other modes of communication. In those cases where the new media acted as a tool of popular mobilization and organization democratizing the "Netizens," lacking a clear vision or at least a contingency plan about how to harness and guide the popular forces being unleashed on the streets of North Africa and the Middle East, some might feel a degree of responsibility for the lives lost, physical destruction, and population displacement. The same moral burden attaches when dissidents, like Iranian blogger Hossein Derakhshan, Belarusian Oleg Bebenin, and Cuban Yoani Sanchez, are encouraged by foreign interlocutors to use social media as political tools only to be tracked, identified, arrested, imprisoned, tortured, and sometimes executed by their governments. In China, new media dissenters must not only fear repression by the world's largest security service, but must overcome cultural fear of chaos as well.[206] Today's "liberation technology" movement is fueled by enthusiasts of connection technologies who still bear the burden of proving that in the long run their actions have done more good than harm.

During the Arab uprisings, the administration seemingly got caught in a vice grip of lending support to long-standing allies or supporting popular movements linked through the new media tools. Demands by human rights activists and democratizers for continued support had generated furious lobbying by Arab governments, Israel, and domestic groups who chastised the U.S. for sending mixed messages and failing to provide leadership. The leaders of the Gulf Cooperation Council, composed of Bahrain, Kuwait, Oman, Qatar, Saudi Arabia, and the United Arab Emirates, for example, initially pressured the USG to use Bahrain as a model to follow in bringing about reform without regional destabilization. The so-called "Bahrain model" of dialoguing with the full society to effect reforms was intensely debated within the administration during the regional crisis. Admiral Mullen and Secretary Gates in the meantime reassured the Saudis and other Arab allies that the U.S. remained a friend and "would live up to its security commitments."[207]

Bahrain, home to the U.S. 5th Fleet, which is responsible for securing the western Indian Ocean, was designated a major non-NATO ally in 2003 and has been the recipient of an estimated $100 million annual payment for military hardware.[208] By 27 February 2011, the administration appeared to be promoting "regime alteration" based on the so-called Bahrain reform model. It meant that, "Instead of pushing for immediate regime change—as it did to varying degrees in Egypt and Libya—the United States is urging protesters from Bahrain to Morocco to work with existing rulers."[209] The national "interest" of maintaining stability appeared to be gaining over the democratization "value." The goal would be to prevent regional destabilization and "help keep longtime allies who are willing to reform in power, even if that meant the full democratic demands of their newly emboldened citizens might have to wait."[210] The plan was partly driven by growing concern about the strategic dislocations from a potential Saudi invasion of Bahrain to prevent a Shiite takeover there, followed by instability in the Saudi kingdom itself. Unfortunately, the Bahrain model soon collapsed after fresh protests by the Shi'a majority led to the deployment of 1,200 Saudi and 800 United Arab Emirates troops in Bahrain over U.S. objections. The government opposition called the foreign troops' presence "an undeclared war" and a "blatant occupation."[211]

The Libyan civil war, the potential destabilization of Bahrain and Saudi Arabia, increasing repression in Syria, the possibility of a Yemeni government collapse with the attendant spread of al-Qaeda affiliates, and increased Iranian influence throughout the region were alarming U.S. policymakers. The ad hoc planning had sought to slow the pace of upheaval and prevent further violence by following a country-by-country approach to reform.[212]

It appeared that "the new technologies have helped to mobilize the populations to action in ways that might not have occurred 20 years go. But in the end, the political rules of the game, which predate the Internet, will remain in force."[213] The political rules of the game dictated that in authoritarian countries, like Libya and Ba'athist Syria, authoritarian leaders like Bashar al-Assad would seek to remain in power through repressive military force.

> ...the new technologies have helped to mobilize the populations to action in ways that might not have occurred 20 years go.

The indisputable fact was that the unrest in North Africa and the Middle East was complicating the SOF mission to fight global terrorism as the terrorist groups gained greater operational freedom.[214] As Tunisia's Zine al-Abidine Ben Ali and Egypt's Mubarak lost their power, the remaining authoritarian leaders redirected their efforts and resources toward coping with their own domestic upheaval. As a result, critical intelligence sharing came to a halt or slowed down as the U.S. tried to identify, contact, and establish working relationships with the new players.[215] The relationship between the United States and friendly Arab countries came under great stress as the U.S. was seen siding with the popular uprisings rather than supporting its authoritarian allies. As democracy-seeking revolts began to turn into sectarian Shiite-Sunni violent confrontations, the leaders of the Arab countries went into survival mode focusing on their ability to stay in power, not on the U.S.-led fight against terror.

Long-standing defense and intelligence partnership arrangements to "swap intelligence, interrogate suspects, train commandos or carry out military strikes" had been established after 9/11 with many of these allies. But the popular uprisings had "knocked out some counterterrorism allies from power, and left others too distracted or politically vulnerable to risk open cooperation with the United States."[216] For example, former Guantanamo detainees who had been released to their homes went missing because intelligence and security partnerships were disrupted.[217] In Tunisia and Egypt, security agencies that cooperated with the Central Intelligence Agency (CIA) were disbanded; in Libya, as the United States sought Gaddafi's ouster those relationships were severed; and those with Yemen weakened as the government fought for its own survival. U.S. CT officials remained very concerned and alarmed as the murky situation exposed vulnerabilities in their system. In Yemen, for instance, President Saleh was so preoccupied with the popular unrest and his own survival that "he no longer uses all of his U.S.-trained counterterrorism forces against al Qaeda (sic)" even though the latter was seeking to overthrow the government by using the popular movements as cover for their activities.[218]

On 26 April, after three months of street confrontations, Saleh and opposition groups appeared to have reached an agreement, brokered by the Gulf Cooperation Council and supported by the U.S. and the EU, under which he would cede power to his vice president within 30 days in exchange for immunity from prosecution. General elections would be held 60 days after the transition of power.[219]

Fighting Extremists with the New Media

The new media is now a weapon in the CT toolkit. The role of the Internet, particularly blogs, as useful information operations weapons has been reviewed by Kinniburgh and Dennin, and it is not within our general purview.[220] Recent media disclosures, however, have exposed how cyber warriors exploit the new media for proactive CT work, and this merits some attention. Cyber Jihadists have relied on the Internet and the new social network-based media to radicalize and recruit new members, provide training materials and information, disseminate propaganda, and organize operations. According to the New York Police Department, the Internet has shortened the "radicalization lifecycle" of homegrown terrorists from months to weeks if not days.[221] In addition to the use of Internet websites, television, radio, films, and other familiar instruments of communication to conduct the "war of ideas" or ideological war, the extremists have been manipulating social media sites. A recent report notes that the Salafi movement recently published the second edition of *Inspire* magazine as an Adobe Acrobat file with password security, entitled "Open Source Jihad." It is presented as a resource manual for Muslim jihadists to train in bomb-making, guerrilla tactics, weapons training, and all jihadist-related activities at home without the risk of foreign travel.[222] A recently disclosed U.S. classified operation seeks to develop software that allows the use of fake online identities or "sock puppets" to influence Internet conversations and spread strategic communications.[223] According to U.S. Central Command (CENTCOM) spokesman Navy Commander Bill Speaks, "The technology supports classified blogging activities on foreign language websites to enable CENTCOM to counter violent extremist and enemy propaganda outside the U.S."[224] When completed, the software would allow the U.S. to "respond to emerging online conversations with any number of coordinated messages, blogposts, chatroom posts and other interventions."[225] According to the statement, the original operation had been revealed in 2010 during oversight testimony by General Petraeus, then commander of CENTCOM, before the U.S. Senate Armed Services Committee. It was part of a vital CT and counter-radicalization program called Operation Earnest Voice (OEV), a psychological operations program to counter the al-Qaeda online narrative presence.[226] In testimony before the Senate committee, General James Mattis, then CENTCOM commander, further explained that OEV sought "to disrupt recruitment and training of suicide bombers; deny safe havens for our adversaries; and counter extremist ideology."[227] What remains undisclosed is what metrics are used to establish success or failure in these operations. As the existence of this type of sensitive technology and its intended uses go viral, it will amount to an invitation to our adversaries and rivals to engage in similar uses, and/or adopt countermeasures, with unknown future consequences for us and the world at large.

The Critique of Soft/Smart Power

It is easier to criticize than to govern. The debate over smart/soft power phraseology masks the fact that despite ideological differences on domestic issues there is significant continuity among the Clinton, Bush '43, and Obama administrations in the conduct of foreign policy. Despite the rhetoric, all three presidents are heirs of Wilsonianism, for they have been trying to make the world safe for democracy—by force, by persuasion, or by Tweet. In other words, there is no clear distinction between soft and smart power, and both parties and administrations have employed it.[228] Indeed, Nye himself clarified that the difference between the two is one of degree since the forms of behavior ranged along a continuum.[229]

As previously noted, the Kroenig study used three case studies to highlight the lack of empirical support behind the soft power theory.[230] A systematic study by Schnaubelt criticizes soft power because it means different things to different people; it fails to meet the criteria for assessing a theory's quality; and because when empirically tested against a hypothesized ability of newly elected President Obama to use his popularity to obtain more troop support from our NATO allies, it failed the test.[231] A broader realist critique by Leslie Gelb, president emeritus of the Council on Foreign Relations, asserts that the five components of the soft power paradigm—ideas, values, culture, leadership, and persuasion—can foster or harm the application of power but do not represent power in the international realm.[232]

Accordingly, *ideals* tend to conflict with responsibilities and interests. Why didn't the Clinton administration's commitment to human rights and democratization translate into an international effort to prevent the Rwandan genocide? During his 25 March 1998 visit to Rwanda, the former president issued what is known as the "Clinton apology" for not acting quickly. But as Samantha Power has documented, the United States in fact did virtually nothing "to try to limit what occurred." Indeed, she points out that staying out of Rwanda was an explicit U.S. policy objective because "most U.S. officials opposed to American involvement in Rwanda were firmly convinced that they were doing all they could—and, most important, all they should—in light of competing American interests."[233]

Values, it is argued, "don't travel well and are therefore difficult for governments to translate into power." Since America does not possess a national consensus on values, "Whose values are to be exported ... ?" Furthermore, Americans "differ wildly among themselves about whether and how to foster these values abroad."[234] Even on fundamental values—e.g. individual freedom, democracy, rule of law, tolerance—there are vast differences among the American public. These differences have become more pronounced as the general population has grown more ethnically and racially diverse.[235]

> Since America does not possess a national consensus on values, "Whose values are to be exported...?"

The argument that *culture* is a source and a means of exercising power seems far-fetched since the USG "does not wield music and movies" and many in this country and around the world do not even share the same views on multiculturalism and tolerance.[236] Moreover, as Colin Gray notes, "culture, and indeed civilization itself, are dynamic, not static phenomena."[237] For instance, since the 1980s, the Kennedy administration late historian Arthur M. Schlesinger had warned about the dangers of multiculturalism and its contribution to the disuniting of America.[238] In Europe, uncontrolled immigration, failure to assimilate minorities, and fears of homegrown extremism recently led the leaders of Germany, Great Britain, and France, to openly reject multiculturalism as a failed concept.[239] Europe cannot tolerate as much diversity as the vaster United States, and because it also has a greater population density the rules must be different. The situation is more difficult when the attempts to extend the national culture to the immigrant populations is resisted and rejected. British Prime Minister David Cameron's rejection of "state multiculturalism" and call for a "muscular liberalism" summarized the conundrum facing Europeans. The failure of Europeans in Sweden, Denmark, and Holland, for instance, to stand up for their own traditional values and national identity has led to the rise of opposing nationalistic right-wing and Islamist populist movements.[240]

As far as *leadership* is concerned, it can be inspirational and a popular president like Franklin D. Roosevelt or Ronald Reagan can produce power abroad.[241] One aspect of then Senator Barack Obama's successful campaign for president was raising expectations among his supporters that his personal narrative as the first biracial African-American president and personal charisma would translate into attractive soft power. It is too early to pass judgment on his presidency, but there are limits to charisma; as Gelb puts it, "Why should foreign leaders be swept off their feet by American presidents' charisma any more than American presidents are carried away by the charm of foreign leaders?"[242] Moreover, as the examples of Franklin D. Roosevelt, Winston Churchill, Martin Luther King, Adolf Hitler, Benito Mussolini, Fidel Castro, and Mao Zedong demonstrate, charisma can be a strong force for both good and evil.[243]

Some have suggested that soft power appears to be a less useful tool of policy than popularly supposed, and the relationship between hard and soft power appears to be "mutually enabling" in the sense that "soft power flows to the owner of hard power."[244]

Defense, diplomacy, and development (the 3Ds) are means to the ends of statecraft as well as "channels by which governments press their agendas onto others."[245] They should not be confused with statecraft itself, which is about "managing reality, coupling ends and means in ways that advance a country's interests."[246] It is the connection between ends and means that determines the character, extent, and manner of actions—whether coercive or persuasive—since they are complementary.

3. American Power Constraints

The Quadrennial Defense Reviews

The Congress mandates the DOD to conduct a comprehensive examination of the national defense strategy, force structure, force modernization plans, infrastructure, budget plan, and other elements of the defense program and policies of the United States every four years. There have been four Quadrennial Defense Reviews (QDRs) with the 2010 QDR being the second during wartime.[247] The 2010 QDR was released amidst the country's greatest recession that has undermined the economic security of many Americans and exposed the limits of the existing American social contract. The widespread hardship caused by double digit unemployment, job losses, stagnant wages, increasing health costs, and rising home foreclosures made it urgently necessary to establish domestic policies to create jobs and restore a sense of economic security. It was estimated that unless drastic economic measures were taken, by FY 2020 the federal debt would be near $26 trillion, or the equivalent of 100 percent of GDP.[248] Defense spending is a target for reductions despite having grown at a lower rate than domestic spending in the last decade.[249]

QDRs are meant to be the DOD's most important planning documents but have been criticized for having historical failings[250] or for "utterly failing to do what it was intended to do."[251] The 2010 QDR, in particular, has been criticized by defense experts who believe that it is a "QDR for all seasons" that suffers from severe strategic limitations because it is not preparing the military to fight the most likely wars and conflicts of the future. In fact, it spent more time on "green energy" and fuel efficiency than on terrorism. [252] Secretary Gates in his important January/February 2009 Foreign Affairs article sought to strike a balance in three areas:

> Between trying to prevail in current conflicts and preparing for other contingencies, between institutionalizing capabilities such as counterinsurgency and foreign military assistance and maintaining the United States' existing conventional and strategic technological edge … and between retaining those cultural traits that have made the U.S. armed forces successful and shedding those that hamper their ability to do what needs to be done.[253]

An analysis comparing the 2010 QDR with the three strategic balancing principles articulated by Secretary Gates argued that the 2010 QDR was "meant to translate Secretary Gates's vision into capabilities and to "re-balance" the DOD "to address today's conflicts and tomorrow's threats."[254] But it was "unclear whether the United States has struck the right balance between winning today's wars and preparing for future conflicts, between manpower and technology, and between what DOD will do and what the rest of the national security community will do to meet current and future challenges."[255]

After reviewing the QDR, the bipartisan Independent Quadrennial Defense Review Panel, jointly appointed by Congress and the Secretary of Defense and led in 2010 by former Defense Secretary William Perry and former National Security Advisor Stephen Hadley, reported that current trends must be reversed because our military situation looks like a forthcoming "train wreck."[256] The reason for the harsh criticism is that the QDRs were intended to be long-term, comprehensive planning instruments that challenged existing thinking and examined long-term risks, capabilities, and resources to develop those capabilities. Instead, they became "explanations and justifications … of established decisions and plans."[257]

In mitigation, they remind us that the "latest QDR is a wartime QDR, prepared by a Department that is focused—understandably and appropriately—on responding to the threats America now faces and winning the wars in which America is now engaged."[258] There remains an urgent need to balance the short-term and long-term perspectives by addressing beyond-the-horizon threats, risks, and capabilities together with the short-term, ongoing wartime focus. The independent review panel felt that there will be an increased demand for U.S. hard power and increased need for the "various tools of smart power," but an element of confusion is that for them, "diplomacy, engagement, trade, targeted communications about American ideals and intentions, development of grassroots political and economic institutions" are the tools of smart power, leaving one to wonder what became of soft power.[259]

An additional issue is raised by those who argue that emphasis on discrete military operations, or the use of just enough military force, to deal with a conflict by minimizing military and civilian casualties has led to more failures than successes. A recent study of 36 U.S. operations over the last two decades indicates that they achieved over half of their military objectives and less than 6 percent of their political objectives.[260] In the case of Iraq, for example, concerns still exist regarding the ability of the Iraqi government to secure the country and maintain its integrity after U.S. combat troops departed. Under the U.S.-Iraq Status of Forces Agreement signed by the Iraqi Presidency Council on 4 December 2008, U.S. combat forces had to withdraw from Iraqi cities by 30 June 2009, and all U.S. forces had to be completely out of Iraq by 31 December 2011.[261] As the DOD reduced its footprint in Iraq, the DOS ramped up to assume responsibility for a host of tasks previously discharged by the military. Budgetary constraints and lack of capacity constitute a serious challenge for DOS and U.S. Agency for International Development (USAID) as it is estimated that for each officer deployed there was a need for 16 private contractors.[262]

In his *Foreign Affairs* article, former Defense Secretary Gates, a Russian expert by training, did not write a "Mr. X" Kennan kind of article examining the nature of the enemy. Instead, its general purpose was to explain the Pentagon's National Defense Strategy and the reprogramming of the Pentagon. While crisscrossing the country to further elaborate on the strategy and its implementation, Secretary Gates and Joint Chiefs of Staff Chairman Admiral Mullen sought to explain the rationale behind their proposed wartime reduction of the force and to define the proper use of the military by stressing the need to give soft power a chance to work in the war against radical extremists.[263] Former USSOCOM Commander Admiral Eric Olson, for his part, addressed the necessity for a balanced approach to irregular warfare and also emphasized that "pure military skill is not enough."[264]

If this concern about bureaucratic restructuring, military spending, policy, and strategy sounds familiar, it is because it harks back to the 1940s and 1950s debates in which Paul H. Nitze and George F. Kennan participated at the genesis of containment. On 8 April 2011, for example, Navy Captain Wayne Porter and Colonel Mark Myckleby, two active duty senior members of the Joint Chiefs of Staff, acting in a "personal capacity" consistent with the public positions of Gates and Mullen, issued a report entitled "A National Strategic Narrative." Published under the pseudonym of "Mr. Y" as a takeoff on George Kennan's 1946 "Mr. X" article, it sought to present a smart-power grand strategy.[265] Like the earlier debate about containment, the report's narrative revolves around issues of setting priorities, properly understanding and responding to the global and regional security environment, the U.S. domestic situation, nature of the enemy, reaching proper capacity, and balancing resources.

Civil-Military Relations and Setting National Priorities: General McChrystal's Departure

For some time now, civil-military relations have been a subject of debate among experts and academics. Democratic theorists agree on the fundamental principle of military subordination to civilian rule. Part of democratic governance of national security is "controlling the sword."[266] Likewise, it is commonly agreed that the civilian leaders should rely on military expertise and experience to make informed strategic and operational decisions particularly in times of conflict and during wartime.[267]

There are two theoretical camps in this area of study—professional supremacists and civilian supremacists. Professional supremacists, like Samuel Huntington, argue that "the primary problem for civil-military relations in wartime is ensuring the military an adequate voice and keeping civilians from micromanaging and mismanaging matters."[268] Civilian supremacists, on the other hand, argue that "the primary problem is ensuring that well-informed civilian strategic guidance is authoritatively directing key decisions, even when the military disagrees with that direction."[269] Balancing civil-military priorities is one aspect of the debates on grand strategy and statecraft as illustrated by the case of General Stanley McChrystal's resignation and retirement under pressure and its aftermath.

On 23 July 2010, at the retirement ceremony of General McChrystal, four-star former commander of U.S. and International Security Assistance Forces (ISAF) in Afghanistan, Defense Secretary Gates heaped praise on him "as one of America's greatest warriors," a consummate Ranger who "possessed one of the sharpest and most inquisitive minds in the Army."[270] Gates did not hold back his admiration and appreciation for the retiring officer's career:

> Over the past decade, no single American has inflicted more fear and more loss of life on our country's most vicious and violent enemies than Stan McChrystal … Commanding Special Operation Forces in Afghanistan and Iraq, Stan was a pioneer in creating a revolution in warfare that fused intelligence and operations.[271]

Yet, a month earlier, President Obama accepted General McChrystal's resignation and replaced him with his superior at CENTCOM General Petraeus, who accepted the demotion in position. McChrystal was not forced into retirement due to policy or strategic differences or poor performance. The cause was due to derogatory comments attributed to him and his staff about the president and civilian counterparts in Afghanistan, ambassadors Richard C. Holbrooke and Karl W. Eikenberry, considered by some to be insubordination.[272]

McChrystal was the second commander in charge of the Afghanistan campaign to depart the job since Obama won the 2008 presidential election. General David McKiernan had been relieved by the president on 12 May 2009, and replaced by McChrystal at the request of Defense Secretary Gates and then Joint Chief of Staff Chairman Admiral Mullen allegedly because McKiernan was too conventional, and new thinking and approaches were needed in Afghanistan.[273] McChrystal was credited with the death of Abu Musab al-Zarqawi, leader of al-Qaeda in Iraq, and represented the desired new unconventional thinking. President Obama could have chosen to censure or issue a gag order to McChrystal, just like President Truman had originally done with General McArthur, but having General Petraeus at hand as an alternate field commander made it both politically and strategically easier for him to allow the general to resign.[274]

In the United States, the doctrine of civilian control over the military is an established constitutional process by which the professional military is subordinate and responsible to the authority of the elected civilian political leadership.[275] The media and the general public rightly focused their attention during the McChrystal situation on the American constitutional principle of civilian control over the military under Article 2 Section 1 of the U.S. Constitution, on the career-ending actions of McChrystal and his lieutenants, as well as on the issues associated with the practice of embedding reporters with the troops. The need for proper handling of the media by the military was emphasized by a subsequent order, issued in an unclassified memo on "Interaction with the Media," by Defense Secretary Gates, establishing that military officials will need Pentagon clearance for interviews and other dealings with reporters. The order had been in the works before the McChrystal situation, but its issuance was accelerated by the Pentagon's unhappiness with the content of the *Rolling Stone* interview and its lack of advanced knowledge. The memo requiring top DOD officials to tell Assistant Defense Secretary Douglas Wilson's office before interviews "or any other means of media and public engagement with possible national or international implications," was soon leaked to *The New York Times* and its contents confirmed by Douglas Wilson and press secretary Geoff Morrell.[276] The main debate at home was over whether the prevailing "population centric" COIN strategy advocated by both Petraeus and McChrystal was the right approach to the war in Afghanistan. As previously noted, in Afghanistan COIN operates on the belief that if the counterinsurgents are able to provide security, development aid, and links between the Afghans and their central government, the insurgents will be denied support.

> The restrictive (rules of engagement) were put in place because of modern COIN doctrine's central tenet: The way to succeed is to win over the population. Because the 'people are the prize,' the theory goes, they must not be unduly offended or harmed. This fundamental imperative is intended to drive all other aspects of the campaign … Despite the increasingly restrictive ROEs (rules of engagement), there were reports that civilian deaths actually increased in 2010 and June and July 2010 were the deadliest months for US forces in the nine-year war.[277]

The subsequent drop in coalition-caused civilian casualties showed that they in fact stemmed from increased restrictions on airstrikes and the use of heavy weapons, while the actual increase in civilian deaths was due to the Taliban using larger explosives and resorting in much greater numbers to assassinations, including public killings of women and children.[278] According to the UN Assistance Mission in Afghanistan, in the first six months of 2010, 1,271 civilians were killed and 1,997 were wounded. The single biggest cause of the increase in civilian casualties was insurgent bombings, including both suicide bombings and homemade bombs, which the military calls improvised explosive devices. Together they caused 557 deaths.[279]

The controversy over population-centric COIN in Afghanistan versus a target-centered CT approach in Afghanistan reflected the internal policy debates among the American foreign policy elites and a general dissatisfaction among the informed public over the apparent lack of an exit strategy. One critic points that "the real story should not be the change in personnel but the continuation of a failed policy."[280] An associated critique came from those who believed that the United States and its allies were taking a one-size-fits-all approach against terrorism and that in Yemen and Somalia, for instance, both the CT and COIN strategies had fueled radicalism and turned wide swathes of the population against the West.[281]

The Afghanistan debate was also indicative of the problems generated by divergences between events on the ground and conceptualizations. The COIN approach, lest one forgets, is not a grand strategy at all but rather a subset of our national security strategy. As applied during the Iraqi "surge," it is the patient tactical implementation of an operational "clear, hold, and build" approach dependent on having "more boots on the ground" and combining fighting the enemy (kinetic operations) with winning the people's "hearts and minds," building civil institutions while providing civilians with the development aid and security needed to carry on with their daily lives. To some realists, however, it seemed that from the beginning U.S. forces were fighting terrorists less and nation-building more.[282] As discussed in the next section, there is a still ongoing controversy over the real role of the Iraqi surge.[283] Nonetheless, the "surge" established General Petraeus's reputation and convinced his supporters, collectively known as the "COINistas," that a similar approach would also work in the neglected Afghanistan theater of operations.

The Military-Civilian Debate over Counterinsurgency and Counterterrorism

General David H. Petraeus, a soldier-scholar with significant combat experience, a doctorate from Princeton, and recognition as a "Top Global Thinker of 2010" by *Foreign Policy* magazine, had been put in charge of the Army Combined Arms Center at Fort Leavenworth, Kansas from late 2005 through February 2007 following a second tour of duty in Iraq. It was in that capacity, and with the cooperation of Marine Lieutenant General James Mattis, who became his replacement as commander of CENTCOM, and retired Army Lieutenant Colonel Conrad Crane, that he had gathered a team of experts including Lieutenant Colonel John A. Nagl and Lieutenant Colonel David Kilcullen. Relying heavily on David Galula's Algerian experience, the team helped produce the 2006 U.S. Army/Marine Corps *Counterinsurgency Field Manual*, FM 3-24.[284] Released in December 2006, FM 3-24 is the official doctrine for U.S. COIN operations and the first field manual ever to be reviewed by *The New York Times* becoming a national bestseller. The manual specified that COIN is those military, paramilitary, political, economic, psychological, and civic actions taken by a government to defeat insurgency.[285]

In 2007, with the level of violence increasing the Bush administration faced a tough decision in Iraq, but General Petraeus convinced the administration that a COIN approach with a "surge" in troops could lead to success. Two goals were being sought—one military and the other political. The military goal was to reduce the unabated violence by increasing force levels, creating tactical alliances with Sunni groups, using COIN tactics against insurgents, and focusing on protecting the population. The political goal was to promote and bring about national reconciliation so Iraq would become a stable ally in the war against extremism.[286] Whether the surge had actually worked in Iraq to stop the violence remains a subject of heated debate since it was the basis for the surge strategy in Afghanistan. Among defense analysts there are those who believe that the Iraqi surge accomplished the first goal,[287] while others are skeptical about whether the surge itself was responsible for the decline in violence,[288] or about its permanence.[289] A majority agrees with the conclusion that the second and most important political goal has not been achieved.[290]

Similarly, not everyone within the military establishment shared a commitment toward institutionalizing COIN as a global strategy based on the Iraq or Afghanistan experience. Secretary Gates noted that "The United States is unlikely to repeat another Iraq or Afghanistan—that is, forced regime change followed by nation building under fire—anytime soon."[291]

Colonel Gian Gentile, an active duty Army colonel who teaches at West Point and is one of the harshest critics of COIN-oriented nation building, believes that the "COINistas" suffer from a form of group-think.[292] On 8 April 2011, an oversight review by the Inspector General of the Defense Department disagreed with the conclusions of the U.S. Army Inspector General Agency investigation of the Rolling Stone case and found no proof of wrongdoing by General McChrystal and his military aides and civilian advisers.[293] McChrystal has described the adaptations and innovations adopted after he took command of COIN operations in Iraq. He summarizes them in the phrase, "it takes a network."[294] Accordingly, when he first assumed command of a U.S. Joint Special Operations Task Force (JSOTF) in October 2003, a review of the enemy and our military forces revealed that "we initially saw our enemy as we viewed ourselves."[295] His planners had begun to map the enemy, al-Qaeda in Iraq led by Abu Musab al-Zarqawi, using the model of a traditional hierarchical military structure. But they realized that the model did not fit because the enemy was a decentralized, flat organization. As he put it, "Over time, it became increasingly clear … that our enemy was a constellation of fighters organized not by rank but on the basis of relationships and acquaintances, reputation and fame … the network is self-forming."[296] What to do? According to General McChrystal, an insight came during a visit to a Special Forces team in Mosul while the city was under the command of then Major General David Petraeus.

> During the visit he drew an hourglass on a yellow legal pad. The top half of the hourglass represented the team in Mosul; the other represented our task force [headquarters]. They met at just one narrow point. At the top, our team in Mosul was accumulating knowledge and experience, yet lacked both the bandwidth and intelligence manpower to transmit, receive or digest enough information either to effectively inform, or benefit from, its more robust task force headquarters … The sketch from that evening—early in a war against an enemy that would only grow more complex, capable and vicious—was the first step in what became one of the central missions in our effort: building the network. What was hazy then soon became our mantra: It takes a network to defeat a network.[297]

In other words, based on a SOF unit's operational experience in the battlefield, General McChrystal and his headquarters drew up a new top-down interagency organizational model to fight the enemy. The challenge was to transform a traditional pyramidal military structure "into a flexible, empowered network."[298] The special operations forward team of 15 men supported by a single intelligence analyst that McChrystal visited in Mosul was, like all the rest distributed throughout Iraq, weakly connected to headquarters; it had "limited bandwidth."[299]

The first adaptation was to create a network by fusing analysts and operators from multiple units and agencies and their institutional cultures by placing them side by side in order to accelerate how intelligence traveled between headquarters and the forward teams. But this was linear thinking and only resulted in the creation of a partial network. This second insight led to another adaptation to build "a true network by connecting everyone who had a role—no matter how small or geographically dispersed, or organizationally diverse they might have been—into a successful COIN operation. We called it, in our shorthand, F3EA: find, fix, finish, exploit, and analyze."[300] Eventually, the "network to defeat a network" model sped up the cycle of COIN operations by combining those who found the enemy and those who fixed the target, with the combat teams who finished the target by capturing or killing him, specialists who exploited the intelligence yielded by the raid, and the intelligence analysts who turned the raw data into usable knowledge.[301] The resulting collaborative warfare by high value target teams of military personnel working with diverse intelligence organizations and interagency cross-functional teams were the so-called "secret weapon" described by Bob Woodward.[302]

The Rand Corporation's John Arquilla had earlier suggested that only a networked military could defeat terrorist networks. For him, terrorist cells could share precise information on a need-to-know basis without a hierarchical structure, thus providing them with the ability to disperse and then "swarm" as in the 9/11 attacks.[303] The new organizational model was tactically successful but had no great strategic impact until it was combined with a corresponding conventional forces bottom-up experimentation with interagency teamwork. Innovative field commanders like Task Force Freedom in Mosul (2004-05) under Major General David M. Rodriguez and Colonel Robert Brown; the 3rd Armored Cavalry Regiment in Tal Afar (2004) under Colonel H.R. McMaster; and the 1st Brigade Combat Team, 1st Armored Division in Anbar Province (2006) under Colonel Sean MacFarland began to integrate interagency high value targeting with COIN principles.[304] General Petraeus and Ambassador Chester Crockett even collocated themselves in order to operate as an interagency high-level command team, and when they "used collaborative warfare more broadly in pursuit of a consistent counterinsurgency strategy, the situation in Iraq turned around dramatically."[305]

In Afghanistan, General McChrystal was given extraordinary leeway in handpicking his corps of subordinates, who were committed to rotate between the United States and Afghanistan for a minimum of three years, and had sought to focus on COIN techniques. His plan was to replicate the Iraq innovations combining the interagency network-centric approach and "fighting like the Taliban" while conducting COIN operations.[306] The press published unconfirmed reports that in the Afghan/Pakistan battle space, USSOCOM had been operating drones and conducted "snatch and grab" and other sensitive operations against high value targets.[307] Nighttime raids had led to complaints about civilian casualties and seemed to be interfering with the COIN attempt to protect and win over the population. Following an unfortunate operation in the village of Kathaba on 11 February 2010 that led to civilian deaths, McChrystal moved to "direct the realignment of all SOF" to his command.[308]

In December 2009, despite some criticism from war opponents and following a lengthy debate within the administration, President Obama announced his decision to partially meet General McChrystal's request for 40,000 more troops to surge in Afghanistan by sending 30,000 additional troops. However, the president was also committed to establishing a withdrawal timeline and established the start date for that withdrawal for July 2011. Subsequently, timetables would be set for transfer of responsibilities to the Afghans and the total withdrawal of U.S. forces. COIN is by definition a long-term human and material capital-intensive approach to asymmetric warfare, and its essence is patience. It requires a whole-of-government approach in which civilian, military, and nongovernmental organizations (NGOs) work in a collaborative manner. The Obama administration's announcement to initially surge but subsequently withdraw American fighting forces from Afghanistan starting in July 2011 raised the possibility of a weakened COIN approach. Domestic politics associated with the midterm election were obviously playing a role as the climbing casualty rate weakened public support; and with the country in the midst of its worst recession ever, here was also talk of reducing military expenditures. More importantly, the timetable

> *COIN is by definition a long-term human and material capital-intensive approach to asymmetric warfare and its essence is patience.*

was criticized for giving the enemy an incentive to wait out the United States and a disincentive to our allies to continue fighting.[309] In fact, on 31 July 2010, the Netherlands was the first NATO ally to withdraw from Afghanistan, thus setting the stage for other allied countries to begin their own departures.

Vice President Biden's Intervention and Counterterrorism

During the 2009 internal policy debate on Afghanistan-Pakistan Vice President Joe Biden, skeptical of a purely COIN/hearts and minds approach succeeding in Afghanistan, had publicly opposed the Petraeus/McChrystal strategy and advocated for a CIA-led CT approach. Counterterrorism is defined as "operations that include the offensive measures taken to prevent, deter, preempt, and respond to terrorism."[310] Biden supported a Pakistan-first approach with a small footprint in both countries, special operations decapitation raids against high value targets, strikes with unmanned aerial systems (e.g. Predator drones), while avoiding nation-building activities. As he put it, "We are in Afghanistan for one express purpose: Al-Qaeda ... Al-Qaeda exists in those mountains between Afghanistan and Pakistan. We are not there to nation-build. We're not out there deciding we're going to turn this into a Jeffersonian democracy and build that country."[311] Biden preferred conducting effects-based intelligence operations by the CIA and special mission units because there was some empirical evidence that leadership decapitation can help to achieve military and political goals.[312] The military leadership persevered by combining the successful CT interagency high value targeting and COIN into a hybrid approach.

As the COIN campaigns in Marja and Kandahar seemed stalemated by the end of summer 2010, Biden's view seemed to regain attention within the administration as the media reported that the CIA continued to create havoc among the enemy by successfully killing terrorist leaders with drone attacks. According to *The New York Times*, the administration's apparent shift in thinking was allegedly reflected in the public remarks of various officials such as incoming commander General James N. Mattis, an advocate of hybrid warfare and supporter of FM 3-24, who when asked whether the July 2011 drawdown date implied a shift from COIN to CT confirmed it by plainly answering, "I think that is the approach, Senator."[313]

CT operations seek to provide a secure environment for governance and development. General Petraeus was well aware of the connection and on 1 August 2010 issued a 24-point guidance entitled "COMISAF's Counterinsurgency Guidance" for the service members and civilians of NATO ISAF and U.S. Forces-Afghanistan."[314] It built upon McChrystal's guidance of November 2009, reinforcing the combined COIN/CT approach while emphasizing the need to "help confront the culture of impunity, identify corrupt officials, and be a good guest."[315] In addition, both publicly and privately Petraeus lobbied against the reduction in the number of troops. As reported in *The New York Times*, while the president's party was pressing for a substantial troop withdrawal, the military leadership asked for more time and flexibility to make the full civil-military COIN campaign succeed.[316]

When to withdraw from Afghanistan?

The controversy over seemingly conflicting timetables was derived from the "two-year rule" presented by Secretary Gates during the review of the Afghanistan/Pakistan strategy. As reported, Gates had argued that "in any particular location you should be able to 'clear, build, hold and transfer' to the Afghan forces within two years" once troops were in place. The two-year clock is said to have initially started in June 2009 when 20,000 additional troops arrived in Afghanistan. However, since U.S. Special Forces operations in the Marja and Kandahar areas had begun later, for them the clock would not stop until 2012.[317] Unforeseeable events intervened, however, that rendered that timetable malleable. First, the 23 June resignation of General McChrystal and his replacement by General Petraeus as commander of the NATO-led ISAF introduced a new dynamic. General Petraeus, a bright, articulate, and politically astute officer with a reputation as a savvy bureaucratic infighter, by accepting the demotion from head of CENTCOM would now see his own Petraeus Doctrine be put to the test in Afghanistan under very difficult conditions. He therefore had a tremendous incentive to succeed, but in order to accomplish it he first had to find a way around the July 2011 deadline to start withdrawing troops.

Second, the results of the November 2010 midterm elections provided the U.S. military with the political opening as President Obama headed to Europe for a NATO meeting. At the two-day NATO summit in Lisbon 19-20 November, the war-weary NATO allies accepted General Petraeus's plan for a troop drawdown starting in July 2011 with the gradual withdrawal of combat troops ending in 2014. The U.S. and its NATO allies adopted a "clear, hold, and hand over" common goal of transferring the lead in the battle against the Taliban to local forces by 2014 and retaining a military presence in the country beyond that date.[318] So it has become a race against the clock. Third, Afghan leaders also balked at the idea of a quick withdrawal in July 2011 for fear that it might start a civil war and allow the Taliban to regain control.[319] The fragility of the Afghanistan mission after a decade is related to a number of factors such as: a resilient Taliban able to operate and recruit among ethnic Pashtuns who are convinced that foreign forces will soon leave; the weakness of the developing Afghan forces due to high levels of illiteracy, corruption, and untrustworthiness, as shown by incidents of rogue soldiers and police turning their weapons against their ISAF mentors; and diminished political support for the state-building effort due to excessive corruption in the system.[320]

American policy toward Afghanistan is to prevent it from again becoming a haven for terrorism while strengthening the central government to keep the Taliban from taking over. General Petraeus during his 15 March 2011 testimony before the Senate Armed Services Committee, acknowledged that "significant progress" had been made in Afghanistan toward completing the "clear, hold, and hand over" NATO transition plan, but that while the security progress achieved over the past year is significant, it is also "fragile and reversible."[321] Reasons for the fragility are the return of al-Qaeda training camps, Taliban resilience, and the pervasiveness of corruption and the drug trade.[322]

Another reason is the tense relationship between the United States and the regime of Afghan President Hamid Karzai. The late Ambassador Richard Holbrooke, for example, had face-to-face verbal clashes with Karzai over his regime's failure to fight corruption and the influence of drug traffickers that were turning Afghanistan into a narco-state.[323] Corruption in Afghan society goes beyond the drug trafficking to include foreign influences like Chinese brothels in Kabul and drinking bars that offend the Muslim faithful and defeat soft power efforts by diminishing the appeal of Western cultural values.[324] In April 2011, Karzai replaced the ministers of defense and finance because he saw them as being too close to the U.S. and its allies.[325] General Petraeus expressed his concerns about maintaining a future presence in Afghanistan before the Senate Armed Services committee—adding that NATO had already signed a Strategic Partnership Agreement with Afghanistan and the U.S.—expected to have a bilateral accord in order to remain involved in Afghanistan post-2014.[326] The implication is an increase in U.S. civilian involvement in Afghanistan, as in Iraq, during the military drawdown.

Bing West calls the COIN strategy being used in Afghanistan a "franchise business and the variations among the franchises is enormous."[327] The strategy being followed, West says, is based on "gratitude theory" or winning hearts and minds, the idea that "if we build enough hospitals and pave enough roads, the Afghan people will stop supporting the Taliban and throw their weight behind the government."[328] Gratitude theory rarely works and most likely it will not in Afghanistan. However, it is also not a characteristic of the present U.S. CT doctrine, and the phrase "hearts and minds" only appears in an appendix of FM-3-24, written by David Kilcullen and explains the true meaning of the approach.[329]

The Modern Solarium "Movement"—Structured Deliberation as a Solution to Civil-Military Issues?

Is it possible to better integrate the art of statecraft with strategic leadership, planning, and implementation? Can we find a better way to avoid America's "chaotic road to war?"[330] The Eisenhower-era Project Solarium exercise is still considered the model for grand strategy development through a process of formal planning and is relevant to current national security challenges. Government declassified documents and subsequent oral histories with participants revealed that in 8 May 1953, a top secret competitive analysis exercise began with three task forces of specialists. Task forces A, B, and C were created and each assigned to examine and propose a separate strategy. They were given access to all available intelligence and asked to study the most likely threats based on a set of assumptions about Soviet capabilities and intentions different from that provided to the other two groups.[331]

George Kennan was made chairman of Task Force A (containment scenario) and assigned to modify, propose new initiatives, and make the best possible argument for Truman's policy of containment. In other words, after being forced out by Secretary of State John F. Dulles, Kennan was called back into government service by Eisenhower to perfect the very strategy that he had fathered. Task Force B (line in the sand) was headed by Air Force Major General James McCormack and tasked with preparing and drawing a perimeter line of U.S. global security interests. His group would argue for making an announcement to the USSR and its allies that crossing the line would constitute an act of war. The United States and its allies would respond with an all-means massive retaliation. Task Force C ("rollback"), led by Vice Admiral Richard L. Connolly and with General Goodpaster, a strong advocate of nuclear deterrence as a group member, was to propose active measures short of war along the whole political, economic, diplomatic, and covert spectrum to dislodge Soviet penetration of the West and weaken Soviet control over Eastern Europe and the Soviet Union itself. In short, it was a "rollback" scenario that Paul H. Nitze had earlier proposed, and Ronald Reagan would revisit decades later, to halt and reverse Soviet occupation of territory.[332] Eisenhower sought to establish a balanced and integrated strategy for the uncertain future through the Solarium exercise, so going forward it is significant that the circumstances faced then parallel the challenges being faced by today's leaders and strategists. The new Solarium movement was led at DOD by then Under Secretary of Defense for Policy Michelle Flournoy, and at DOS by Anne-Marie Slaughter. Prior to joining the Obama administration, both had cooperated in a study of U.S. national strategy drawing inspiration from Eisenhower's Solarium. The main problem identified in the study was that the United States was "lacking both the incentives and the capacity to support strategic thinking and long-range planning in the national security arena."[333] U.S. leaders did not have interagency processes that allowed them to look over the horizon to identify threats, opportunities, and get the whole picture, so ad hocism prevailed; "America's most fundamental deliberations are made in an environment that remains dominated by the needs of the present and the cacophony of current crises."[334] Solarium exercises were proposed not just to improve interagency cooperation but with the end goal "to institutionalize a process for strategy formulation by introducing discipline and systematization to guide statecraft."[335] The expectation was that beginning with the Obama administration, the White House would practice better statecraft by using all the tools in the toolbox more holistically and efficiently.

Since the Eisenhower years, the report continued; strategic planning had declined in subsequent administrations due to three trends:

> First, the special assistant to the president for national security affairs evolved into a powerful political player who, in turn, has helped push the NSC staff to a dominant position in the foreign policy process. Second, informal methods of presidential decision-making ... have tended to eclipse the more structured and formal mechanisms that were once equally valued and prominent in the process. Finally, as presidential administrations have focused on crisis management and daily operations, outside entities, such as Congress, other government agencies, and think-tanks, have attempted to address the strategic planning deficit, with varying results. These trends run deep in the currents of national security policy and process and have greatly influenced American foreign policy development over the last fifty years.[336]

At the heart of the issue was how to deal with the extant institutionalized groupthink mentality within the foreign policy establishment. To address the problem set a strategic planning process was proposed with three key elements: conduct a quadrennial national security review (QNSR), establish an interagency threat assessment process to support the QNSR, and establish a resource allocation process. In addition, three process-oriented solutions are suggested within the ambit of organization theory.[337] Flournoy's study focused on interagency processes and the need to institutionalize Solarium-type exercises, but the weakest link was the main player—the chief executive and commander in chief. The main driver of the Eisenhower Solarium was Eisenhower himself, a president with the experience, commitment, judgment, and skills set to get the job done; but since then no president has sought to perform a similar role.[338]

General Douglas MacArthur allegedly had once said that Ike "was the best clerk he ever had," thereby leaving the false impression that Eisenhower, albeit a great planner, did not have the wherewithal to be a grand strategist. But the record is clear that by the time he assumed the presidency, Ike had amassed a tremendous amount of experience as a strategic leader in both the military and civilian arenas. He had indeed served as chief of staff in the Philippines under General MacArthur, but had also gone from being 64th in his graduating class at West Point to first in his class at the elite Command and General Staff School and eventually supreme commander of one of the greatest military operations—Operation Overlord, the invasion of Europe through Normandy (D-Day) that began on 6 June 1944. After the war, he served as president of Columbia University, and as U.S. president he socially transformed America by creating the interstate highway system and enforcing U.S. Supreme Court desegregation orders in the South. He was, in fact, a diplomat/soldier, a statesman, and man of intellect, extraordinary talent, and character.[339] Unfortunately, even though Ike introduced the Solarium process, he did not institutionalize it at the highest level of government. It was a loss to the future of the country because as he warned in his farewell address, it was necessary to achieve a proper balance between the civilian, military, and economic sectors of the government. As the Cato Institute reminds us:

> Some of the most acrimonious debates within the Eisenhower administration pitted the president against his former colleagues in the

uniformed services. Eisenhower's attempts to adapt military force structure to a new national security strategy became highly politicized, and ultimately failed. Eisenhower was especially worried that future presidents, lacking his military credentials and deep knowledge of national security matters, would be even less willing and able to confront the military. Historically, it raises an important question in the civilian-military relationship regarding whether a commander-in-chief lacking military experience can prevail over uniformed officers who are national figures in their own right?[340]

One expectation was that with Flournoy and Slaughter serving in the Obama administration in key policy positions a formal Solarium process might be institutionalized to provide a president lacking military experience with a roadmap to prevail over uniformed officers who are national figures and use the tools for foreign policy and national security policymaking—i.e. to craft a grand strategy. The resignation of McChrystal, the firing of his predecessor, and the deployment of Petraeus to Afghanistan might have been part of Obama's attempt to prevail over the "uniforms" by showing them who is boss.[341] Unfortunately, it is apparent from insider reports leaked to the media that the Libyan crisis was handled in the same ad hoc way criticized by Flournoy. Referring to the coalition differences over who in NATO should take the lead in the Libyan military operation, Secretary Gates said, "This command-and-control business is complicated, and we haven't done something like this kind of on-the-fly before."[342] But, flying by the seat of the pants is not what we would expect if the U.S. had structured a process to implement a grand strategy.

Balancing strategy: The DOD and DOS Relationship and Smart Power

The absence of an executive-driven, institutionalized Solarium interagency process was mitigated by the collaborative partnership between Secretary Gates at DOD and Secretary Clinton at the DOS. Secretary Gates's emphasis on achieving a balanced strategy refers to the issue of lack of capacity at both DOS and USAID that has led to a corresponding "militarization of foreign policy."[343] The main concern was that military personnel were performing tasks for which their civilian counterparts, with greater training and reach back to civilian agencies, could perform much more effectively.[344] Secretaries Gates and Clinton displayed an unusual unity of effort that filtered down to their two departments. Their personal relationship was paralleled by the relationship that existed between Michelle Flournoy and Anne-Marie Slaughter. The two had previously worked together at the Princeton Project on National Security and at the Center for a New American Security. As a result, the DOD gained a key interagency partner in the DOS and vice versa. One consequence is that Congressional funding to increase capacity in spending and hiring of foreign service officers by the DOS and the USAID has been encouraged and supported by Secretary Gates and the Pentagon chiefs. The move to strengthen the foreign policy civilian arm of the government had actually begun under the direction of President Bush and Condoleezza Rice's "transformational diplomacy," but it continued in earnest under Secretary Clinton.[345]

Secretary Gates proposed that the two departments adopt a "pooled resources" approach when responding to situations where their missions will overlap. Testifying on 16 and 17 March 2011 before the House and Senate Armed Services Committees respectively, he and Admiral Mullen presented a new proposal to fund security sector assistance and stabilization.[346] A new Global Security Contingency Fund was proposed as a way for the DOD to coordinate better with the DOS on civilian support for overseas operations. The fund was to prepare for emerging threats or unforeseen problems and would be seeded with $50 million from the DOS's budget and supplemented with a request to transfer $450 million from the DOD if authorized by Congress.[347] The balanced strategy proposed by Secretaries Gates and Clinton focused on the global environment which had to be stabilized and shaped to make it inhospitable to violent extremism. This would be a population-centric approach focusing on the root causes of global problems and their interconnections. To promote a hospitable environment, the strategy would engage the world using the 3Ds. The balanced strategy would be an integrated DOD/DOS effort using two approaches: a direct and an indirect approach. The direct would be used to isolate the threat in order to defeat it and prevent its reconstitution or reemergence. Isolation of the threat means disruption of violent extremist organizations (VEOs) and denying their access to and use of WMDs. The indirect approach was the preferred method, and it would seek to increase friendly freedom of action and reduce enemy freedom of action by enabling partners while deterring and eroding support for VEOs.[348]

The Quadrennial Diplomacy and Development Review: Building Capacity in the DOS

One change at the DOS, following a 17-month review of U.S. development and diplomacy policies, is the production of the first QDDR.[349] Modeled after the DOD's QDR, the DOS-QDDR is a planning guide that seeks to build American civilian power and provide funding, guidance, and the authorities for DOS and USAID participation in "whole-of-government" activities in the exercise of national power. To a large extent, the QDDR is an overly ambitious attempt to institutionalize the soft power approach by putting more DOS and USAID "wingtips on the ground."[350] Dr. Slaughter also co-directed the DOS new plan to fulfill its role as the diplomatic and civilian arm of the government in foreign policy. A renowned advocate of using international relations theory in the application of international legal theory, it is unclear in what manner and to what extent her preferences in this area are reflected in the QDDR.[351] The United States' investment in blood and treasure both in Iraq and Afghanistan, and whatever rebalancing of military and civilian tasks and budgets may be in the pipeline, are being affected by the mass turmoil in the Middle East and North Africa. Moreover, some of the main players changed roles or left office—Senator Chuck Hagel replaced Leon Panetta in early 2013 as Secretary of Defense. Panetta had replaced Robert Gates in 2012. Additionally, Chairman of the Joint Chiefs of Staff Admiral Mullen retired at the end 2011, and Secretary Clinton was replaced by Senator John Kerry in early 2013. So efforts to balance DOD and DOS and collective plans to balance the military and civilian sectors of the government are entering a severe time of testing.[352]

4. USSOCOM and Soft Power

USSOCOM and the War Against Terror[353]

In the global confrontation against terrorist networks, radical extremists, transnational criminal organizations, and other non-state and state adversaries, SOF are at the tip of the spear. USSOCOM was activated on 16 April 1987 at MacDill Air Force Base, Florida, in response to the Congressional Goldwater-Nichols Defense Reorganization Act of 1986 and the Nunn-Cohen Amendment to the National Defense Authorization Act of 1987 (P.L. 99-661). To carry out its mission, Congress provided USSOCOM with specific authorities and responsibilities under Title 10 of the U.S. Code. Under the statute, "The principal function of the command is to prepare special operations forces to carry out assigned missions."[354] Congress mandated a new four-star command with service-like authorities and unique responsibilities for a unified command. USSOCOM is almost like a fifth service; it has its own acquisition authorities to develop and purchase special operations-specific equipment, supplies, and services.[355]

USSOCOM is a unique unified supported and combatant command to plan, synchronize, and execute antiterrorist strategy and operations. The unified command plan has two missions—as a force provider and as the lead combatant command for planning, synchronizing, and as directed, conducting DOD operations against terrorist networks. It serves "in many ways as an extension of the Joint Staff, in some ways as an extension of the Office of the Secretary of Defense."[356] It is composed of the headquarters and the force. Headquarters is the strategic center for determining how special operations ought to be developed and used. In other words, USSOCOM "organizes, trains, and equips Special Operations Forces ... provides those forces to the geographic combatant commanders under whose operational control they serve," and the command "also develops special operations strategy, doctrine and procedures ... and develops and procures specialized equipment for the force."[357]

Throughout U.S. military history, elite troops and special mission teams have been recruited, trained, and organized on an ad hoc basis during wartime to perform special tasks and missions. SOF and their predecessors were not given top priority for most of their history and underwent ups and downs, being underused or misused, valued or underappreciated.[358] For example, during World War II the Army Rangers, tracing their ancestry to the Robert Rogers' Rangers of the American Revolution and established along the tradition of British Commandos, first entered and distinguished themselves in combat, while the Office of Strategic Services (OSS), the military predecessor of the CIA, was tasked to conduct espionage and special operations. At war's end, as the country demobilized, most of these units were disbanded and/or their members returned to their parent services. The OSS, for instance, was split on 20 September 1945 by President Harry S. Truman's Executive Order #9621 (Order effective 1 October 1945) between the DOS and the Department of War.[359] Therefore, the creation of USSOCOM was a sea change in SOF history as it became a permanent headquarters for special operations with a dedicated budget, a command that provides the wherewithal for SOF to develop and operate their missions and roles.

Before 9/11, USSOCOM's primary focus was "on organizing, training and equipping special operations forces and providing forces to support the geographic combatant commanders … it also supported U.S. ambassadors and their country teams."[360] The operational force deployed about 25 percent of the time serving in 120 to 140 countries around the world. These deployments, however, were by small units and of a short term. Early in the George W. Bush administration, then Defense Secretary Donald Rumsfeld had sought to modernize and transform DOD, among other things, by linking "'stove piped' processes into a system-of-systems using a Training Transformation program."[361] The institutional changes began to accelerate in 2004, with SOF heavily engaged in both Afghanistan and Iraq, when Rumsfeld expanded USSOCOM's responsibilities to include synchronization of DOD's planning for global operations against terrorism. Synchronization meant that USSOCOM would be a force provider synchronizing the planning of operations, while the geographic combatant commanders would synchronize, or be responsible, for carrying out the operations.[362]

> …USSOCOM would be a force provider synchronizing the planning of operations while the geographic commanders would synchronize, or be responsible, for carrying out the operations.

In 2008, DOD further expanded USSOCOM's brief by designating it as the joint "proponent" for security force assistance (SFA). Proponent means that the command helps policymakers by prioritizing requirements regarding "which potential partner nations the U.S. military ought to work with, in what priority, and in what manner ... and make recommendations to the Joint Staff regarding which special operations forces, which general purpose forces or which combination of forces are most appropriate ... "[363] SFA is an expansion of USSOCOM's foreign internal defense mission based on a mix of SOF, conventional forces, and other relevant agencies.[364] This was followed by DOD Directive 3000.07 (4) (a) of 1 December 2008, that recognized "that [irregular warfare] is as strategically important as traditional warfare."[365] USSOCOM has capitalized in this new way of thinking to increase and firm up its institutional position, roles, mission, and budgets.

Former USSOCOM Commander Admiral Olson oversaw the rapid expansion of SOF while managing a DOD Major Force Program-11 (MFP-11) budget with a request for $10.5 billion in FY 2012. The MFP-11 is provided to the commander of USSOCOM to address requirements that are "SOF-peculiar" in nature.[366] On 5 May 2008, in his first public statement as commander of USSOCOM, Admiral Olson had noted that SOF were so heavily engaged in the wars in Iraq and Afghanistan that they were spread thin and unable to fully perform traditional roles elsewhere. The Spanish language proficient U.S Army 7th Special Forces Group (Airborne), based in Fort Bragg, North Carolina, for instance, whose area of focus is Latin America, had taken two of its three battalions to the Middle East, leaving them "underrepresented in Latin America."[367] Before 9/11, 20 to 25 percent of the force was deployed to the Middle East, but since March 2003, about 80 percent of the forces were deployed to the CENTCOM region.[368] The Arab Spring upheavals in Northern Africa and the Middle East, coupled with the decision to intervene in the Libyan civil war, suggest that SOF deployments in the U.S. Africa Command (AFRICOM) area of responsibility (AOR) will grow, but the imbalance toward the CENTCOM AOR probably will continue for the foreseeable future even as conventional forces depart Iraq and Afghanistan. As a result of the increased missions and roles, USSOCOM's budget doubled between 2001 and 2005 and was set to increase by 50 percent under the 2006 QDR.

The 2006 QDR included a number of decisions that affected the nature and composition of the force. In particular, it sought to remedy the SOF personnel problem by increasing its size by 13,000 (33 percent) over a five-year period and instituting the 18X program under which qualified recruits were allowed to enter directly from civilian life.[369] During Admiral Olson's tenure, SOF grew in numbers and was in such high demand that it raised a new set of challenges. By 2011, the force totaled about 60,000 people with one third composed of "careerists," or those who have been "selected, trained and qualified to earn the Military Occupational Specialty or skill code identifier of a SOF operator."[370] Half of the force was added since 9/11 with an average age of 30, of which 70 percent are married. Under a DOD pilot recruiting program called Military Accessions Vital to the National Interest (MAVNI), visa holders with two or more years of residence in the U.S. and medical, foreign language, or cultural skills essential to national security were eligible to expedite naturalization by enlisting in the Army. One third of the applicants thus recruited expressed an interest in joining SOF.[371]

USSOCOM's primary focus prior to 11 September 2001 was on organizing, training, and equipping SOF and providing forces to support the geographic combatant commanders, but over the past decade SOF grew in "manpower, budget allocation, (and) overall capacity by virtue of their expanded force, work volume, and level of achievement."[372] SOF's innate capabilities, skills set, and force structure were exceptionally suited to engage the globally diverse, networked, technologically savvy, astute, asymmetric adversaries of the United States. Growth when properly managed is desirable, but it has a downside; the increased volume of work, for instance, may lead to overuse or misuse, raising issues of force depletion, desertion, or preservation of standards to remain mission proficient.[373]

Such a rapid growth also seemed to violate the SOF Truths that "SOF cannot be mass produced" and "quality is better than quantity."[374] USSOCOM headquarters was therefore left with the challenge of implementing the unprecedented growth through proper recruitment, assessment, selection, and arduous training of the new personnel while managing force sustainment—i.e. force rotation and regeneration while sustaining an operational presence—at a high operational tempo and maintaining SOF-unique qualities and capabilities.[375] Nonetheless, according to Admiral Olson, "retention rate is higher than it has ever been; recruiting is pretty good; we are growing … all at an unprecedented rate," but "our ability to absorb growth is limited to the 3 to 5 percent range because of our internal structures and our need to not lose our soul in the process of growth."[376]

SOF have a worldwide mission, and the extended deployments to the CENTCOM AOR reduced capacity in the other geographic combatant commands leaving 6 percent in the U.S. Pacific Command, 4 percent in AFRICOM, 2 percent in the U.S. European Command, 2 percent in the U.S. Southern Command, and less than 1 percent in the U.S. Northern Command AOR.[377] The intensive deployment and growth of SOF has been of such unprecedented size, duration, and repeat rotation that SOF have been operating with conventional forces for extended periods of time and are increasingly unable to meet the new global demand for their services without the enabler and logistics support provided by the conventional forces. Conventional forces, for example, provide SOF with "basing, messing, fuel, motor pools, medical facilities, ammunition resupply, and base security."[378] Admiral Olson confirmed this mutual interdependence by resurrecting the fifth SOF Truth that "Most special operations require non-SOF support."[379] As a result, the 2010 QDR report directed an increase of key enabling assets, maintaining approximately 660 special operations teams, increasing civil affairs capacity, and several other changes aimed at supporting the command.[380]

Direct and Indirect Approaches in USSOCOM

USSOCOM's core special operations tasks or activities within DOD include direct action, CT, counter-proliferation of WMDs, unconventional warfare, foreign internal defense, SFA, civil-military operations, military information support operations, information operations, COIN, special reconnaissance, and the catch-all, "other activities as may be specified by the secretary of defense of the president."[381] The DOD campaign strategy in countering violent extremism (CVE) is a Concept Plan (CONPLAN) 7500 supported by regional plans by each of the geographic combatant commanders. Admiral Olson has sketched CONPLAN 7500 as establishing two interdependent approaches to CVE: the direct and the indirect. Direct actions are:

> Short duration strikes and other small-scale offensive actions conducted as a special operation in hostile, denied, or politically sensitive environments and which employ specialized military capabilities to seize, destroy, exploit, recover, or damage designated targets. Direct action differs from conventional offensive actions in the level of physical and political risk, operational techniques, and the degree of discriminate and precise use of force to achieve specific objectives.[382]

According to Admiral McRaven, they are "precision, highly kinetic strike force" missions.[383] Direct actions are mostly urgent, necessary, chaotic, kinetic, quick, and measurable fighting missions to interdict, kill, or capture terrorists, their facilities, their organizations and destroy their support networks. In the public's mind, direct action is traditionally associated with the work of commandos. The U.S. military is in the lead on the direct approach, and the effects are "almost always near-term and short-lived."[384] While the direct approach seeks to isolate the threat, the indirect approach refers to:

> The application of military and non-military action by, with and through partner nations to influence, neutralize or defeat an enemy by shaping the physical and psychological environment in which he operates. It may include kinetic actions at the tactical level to kill an enemy and/or disrupt his plans and operations. The indirect approach requires whole-of-U.S. government effort in its application.[385]

The indirect approach seeks "to shape and influence the environment."[386] People, units, and capabilities cannot be categorized as being one or the other, but on the indirect approach, as Admiral Olson plainly put it, "the United States military is, to a large degree, pushing from behind."[387] The two approaches are mutually supportive with the strike capability providing space and time for indirect efforts to work.[388]

The Indirect Approach

The National Defense Authorization Act of 2005, Section 1208, is a key tool that provides the authorities and funds for the training and equipping of regular and irregular indigenous forces to conduct CT operations.[389] Unlike the indirect approach, the direct approach is seldom by itself decisive.[390] According to Admiral Olson, "enduring results come from indirect approaches."[391] The indirect approach involves a complex set of activities that include identifying and recruiting the appropriate indigenous persons that can be leveraged by SOF to increase their understanding and effectiveness in working within the local environment. It means organizing parallel organizations to compete with existing terrorist networks with the collaboration of interagency, multinational, and/or nongovernmental partners— i.e. a whole-of-government approach. It also means engaging in proactive intelligence collection[392] through a deep sociocultural understanding and social penetration of terrorist networks that operate in "plain sight" as well as eliminating the environment in which terrorists are produced and recruited. It also includes preparation of the environment in Phase 0 or "non-war" and "preventive war" situations by engaging in activities associated with soft power approaches.[393]

The strategy of indirect approach is attributed to B.H. Liddell Hart who in 1929 under the title *The Decisive Wars of History* included it in the preface to his *Strategy of the Indirect Approach*.[394] As he later explained, "The true aim is not so much to seek battle as to seek a strategic situation so advantageous that if it does not of itself produce the decision, its continuation by a battle is sure to achieve this."[395] For Liddell Hart, the strategic objective should be to take the initiative from the enemy by *dislocating* the organization of his attack, *disrupting* his scheme of maneuver, and *neutralizing* the power of his forces.[396]

The Liddell Hart indirect approach strategy is in fact a Western adaptation of Sun Tzu's *Art of War* call for armies to advance along the lines of least expectations against the enemy's line of least resistance. Sun Tzu emphasized that the greatest virtue was defeating your enemies indirectly because you could protect your resources while depleting those of your adversary. Ralph D. Sawyer's excellent work breaks down Sun Tzu's fundamental principles into four contemporary basic themes that address the direct and indirect approaches: fundamentals, command and control, important strategies and methods of warfare, and tactical principles.[397] It is in the third theme of strategies and methods that Sun Tzu more directly addresses the indirect approach in terms of selecting the most advantageous terrain, deceiving your enemy by hiding your true intentions, and using all the elements of power (e.g. military, diplomatic, economic) to build alliances and influence the people's will.[398] The objective was to direct the major efforts toward the points of least resistance to capture the weakest links.

Major General Bennet S. Sacolick, then-commander, John F. Kennedy Special Warfare Center and School, wedded the indirect approach to President Obama's foreign policy when he said, "I believe that a strategy of global engagement employing Special Forces soldiers, may be our best bet at winning this War. Terrorist organizations like the Taliban, Al-Qaida (sic), Hamas, and Hezbollah must be defeated at the local, grass roots-level by a combination of development, diplomacy and defense, hence global engagement."[399] Using the Army Special Forces indirect activities in Afghanistan as an example, Sacolick adds:

> Less than 8 percent of our overall force structure belongs to a Special Operations Task Force. In one recent six-month rotation, these Special Operators conducted hundreds of operations, engaging and killing thousands of Taliban insurgents. However, what is most noteworthy is that they also medically treated more than 50,000 Afghanis, delivered over 1.4 million pounds of aid, and established over 19 radio stations. They also distributed 8,000 radios, so the country's populace can now listen to an Afghani voice of reason as opposed to extremists ranting of anti-American, Taliban rhetoric.[400]

A recent study by Thomas H. Henriksen examined several cases where the U.S. has used the indirect approach and cautions against applying a universal model for an indirect approach to COIN. In Vietnam, the indirect approach consisted of training and equipping Montagnard tribes for local self-defense and as surrogates in strike operations against the Vietcong/North Vietnamese forces. But ethnic and cultural differences and antagonism between the Montagnards and the South Vietnamese interfered with their integration into the central government forces. Similarly, in Somalia the indirect approach relied on using local warlords as surrogates against VEOs to seize or assassinate suspects. The result, however, was a decline in the legitimacy of COIN efforts among the population due to U.S. association with unsavory groups. In contrast, the indirect approach has succeeded in the Philippines government COIN campaign against Abu Sayyaf and other insurgents. In that theater of operations, SOF have worked with the government, first, in an indirect support capacity to rescue hostages; and later, by training and mentoring Philippine forces while avoiding direct combat participation with the insurgents. The lesson learned from the Philippine experience was that due to the unique historical, political, and social characteristics of the country, the experience could not be readily transferred to other conflicts. In other words, the application of the indirect approach is a command decision that requires a wise case-by-case implementation.[401]

This command decision aspect is critically important since it is the current view that the indirect approach ultimately leads to decisive effects on the battlefield while the direct approach only buys time.[402] Yet, according to Malvesti,

Many policymakers at all levels of government lack an understanding of the full range of SOF capabilities … they tend to equate special operations with … the direct approach—almost exclusively with, kind of, the snatch-and-grab missions, efforts to rescue hostages, takedowns, other kinetic-type operations. And they tend to be unaware of the SOF warrior-diplomat role … the unique, culturally attuned capabilities that special operations forces bring to bear, particularly in working with relevant populations. And this really is a missed opportunity.[403]

The Democratic Republic of the Congo: SOF as Armed Humanitarians Advancing a Global Social Agenda?

An example of how the new global agenda challenges SOF capacity is found in the Democratic Republic of the Congo (DRC), formerly Zaire, a state in Central Africa. The DRC has the potential to be one of the richest countries in the world due to the vastness of its natural resources. It has more arable land than the PRC, and possesses diamonds and minerals like tin, tungsten, tantalum, and gold that are essential to manufacture cell phones, laptop computers, digital cameras, and other products.[404] From August 1998 to July 2003, the country was devastated as nine African nations—Rwanda, Libya, Sudan, Burundi, Tanzania, Angola, Namibia, Zambia, and Zimbabwe—and dozens of armed tribal and ethnic groups fought the "Great War of Africa" or "Second Congo War" within its territory. It was the largest war in African history and the deadliest since World War II with over 5.5 million people dead from the hostilities, disease, and starvation while millions more were displaced or forced to migrate.[405]

The DRC is a key to stability in the central African region because it borders nine different states. Since 2003, international humanitarian and development efforts led by the Country Assistance Framework of the United Nations and the World Bank have followed.[406] In FY 2010 alone, the U.S. provided $306 million in bilateral assistance programs through the DOS and USAID to support economic growth, education, health, and other critical sectors.[407] The DRC remains challenged by a host of structural, socioeconomic, and governance problems. Tribal and militia fighting, corruption, and institutional weakness limit the government's ability to tackle the trade in conflict minerals, human trafficking, children armies, illiteracy, malnutrition, and rape. Violent groups like the Liberation Forces for the Liberation of Rwanda continue to operate within Congo. A sort of limited war has also raged for 23 years in the DRC with the Lord's Resistance Army (LRA), a militia group that fled Uganda and moved to the border area with the DRC. Known for committing atrocities, the LRA was confronted by the Armed Forces of the Democratic Republic of Congo (FARDC) who were sent to garrison the area. Unfortunately for the people of the region, due to indiscipline, instead of protecting the population the soldiery allegedly also began committing acts of mass and individual rapes. Police and private citizens too were accused of participating in the thousands of violent rapes that occur in the country every year. As U.S. Principal Deputy Assistant Secretary of State Donald Yamamoto has testified, there are "numerous instances when state security forces are the ones who commit abuses against Congolese civilians."[408] According to a senior official at the UN, the DRC is the "rape capital of the world."[409]

During a 2009 visit to Congo, Secretary Clinton met with rape victims and was so emotionally touched that she pledged $17 million in assistance to prevent sexual and gender-based violence. She promised to bring American power to bear on the culture of rape. At the time, critics felt that she had responded with a "soft" approach to the problem by unveiling a minimalist plan to build health clinics and supply rape victims with video cameras to document the violence. Later on, she concluded that only the military could address an issue of such magnitude and turned to the successful security-sector development approach being used by the U.S. military in Iraq and Afghanistan. The goal of a security sector approach is to rebuild the local army and police forces and then have so-called "advise and assist" brigades be temporarily assigned to help the local brigades formed by the U.S. over the years. With the cooperation of Secretary Gates, Secretary Clinton made a commitment to provide Congo with a similar program. Soon thereafter, in December 2009, the commanders, staff officers, and noncommissioned officers of a new light infantry battalion began training in Kisangani, Congo.[410]

AFRICOM, through its special operations component, Special Operations Command - Africa, provides on-the-ground oversight of the training program taught by U.S. military personnel and DOS contractors.[411] Before the Libyan intervention, AFRICOM had taken the task very seriously and made the program a priority item. American military instructors had the tall order of learning new skills like rape-prevention and integrating sexual-violence prevention into the training of Congolese forces. What makes it a tall order is that, first, they had to get rogue elements of the Congolese Army itself to stop raping, and then send them to protect civilians from groups such as the LRA.[412] Next, they had to "train the trainers" before deploying them to work with the rest of the force. The U.S. Special Forces and DOS personnel will seek, among other things, to bring about military reform by training a model light infantry battalion of 750 Congolese soldiers to conduct internal security operations and seed the rest of the Congolese Army with Western values regarding sexual violence, protection of civilians, and respect for human rights and international law. On 17 February 2010, during the welcoming ceremony at Kisangani, Ambassador William Garvelink, U.S. Ambassador to the DRC, stated, "The United States of America and the Democratic Republic of Congo are committed to a partnership to train and professionalize a FARDC battalion that will respect and protect the Congolese people."[413] Another issue is that Congo is categorized by the DOS as a "Tier 3" country, or one whose government does not fully comply with U.S. minimum standards for the elimination of human trafficking, and is not making significant efforts to do so. Therefore, without also raising the social status of women throughout Congolese tribal and ethnic society, any efforts to protect them from institutionalized rape by seeding a discrete military sector might prove ephemeral.[414]

This Congo mission is obviously different from traditional military missions to advance American interests by strengthening alliances, building partner capacity, and providing humanitarian relief. For example, in the Western Hemisphere, the U.S. Southern Command and the U.S. Navy's 4th Fleet in the past years have executed a mission program entitled Operation Continuing Promise (OCP). A Bush administration initiative, OCP is a highly successful program of humanitarian and civic assistance to provide access to quality health, dental, and veterinary care at no cost, while sharing healthcare knowledge and best practices with local healthcare providers in eight Caribbean and Latin American countries. It is a limited, time-constrained operation that does not expose American military personnel to kinetic encounters or direct combat operations and has a multiplier effect in terms of goodwill.[415] The Congo mission, by comparison, has not resulted in a major turnaround. A forthcoming study in the *American Journal of Public Health* reports that 1,152 women are raped daily in the Congo—or the equivalent of 48 per hour. In a 12-month period between 2006-2007 the total number of rape victims reached 400,000.[416]

In sum, in the DRC under the rubric of smart power, SOF are deployed as "armed humanitarians" not to fight or to help build partner-nation capacity or to combat terrorist networks but rather to handle an endemic social problem.[417] The lack of capacity in the DOS and USAID has meant that the DOD has borne the brunt of these types of missions. This "militarization of foreign policy" is bound to continue due to recent cuts in DOS and USAID funding that will cement their lack of expeditionary capacity. By virtue of identifying universal human rights as being similar to national interests, the U.S. risks turning peripheral interests into vital ones.[418]

Whether using the military to conduct social engineering as a form of foreign policy (i.e. smart power) generates goodwill and acceptance rather than resentment and more insecurity for the American people at home,[419] or whether the warrior ethos can be maintained as combat training time is traded for tackling poverty, bridging divides, serving children in crisis, changing cultural norms and values, building institutions, and a host of other civilian missions remain open questions.[420] As discussed in the next section, these issues of capabilities and cost-benefit concerns take the form of calls for a balanced strategy.

A Question of Balance

Balanced warfare is therefore the way SOF are combating terrorism and the guiding principle behind the DOD's CONPLAN-7500 to combat global terrorist networks. It calls for the careful balancing of the direct and indirect approaches. Admiral Olson, commenting on balanced warfare, has said, "It is easy on paper but difficult in practice."[421] While the direct approach seeks to capture, kill, interdict, and disrupt terrorists and their networks, the indirect approach is made up of those actions in which SOF support and enable partner nations to fight VEOs. As expressed by Lieutenant General David P. Fridovich, U.S. Army, retired, former USSOCOM deputy commander:

> We contribute to our partner-nation's capabilities by advising, training, equipping, transferring technology and combat monitoring the partner nation's military forces. The indirect approach includes efforts … where a government is either unwilling or unable to eliminate terrorist sanctuaries … The indirect approach requires a whole-of-government effort to attack the underlying causes of terrorism.[422]

SOF are operating on "an unprecedented scale across the globe … but are not yet optimized for success."[423] In addition to the challenges presented by more than nine years of sustained combat operations and the growth experienced across the board—ranging from larger budgets and a wider spectrum of missions to a larger force—USSOCOM faces challenges associated with the lack of a national grand strategy that guides and prioritizes the use of force, in particular the use of SOF, in order to achieve strategic effects.

Split the Force?

The ongoing debate over conventional military forces becoming more "SOF-like" overlaps another about the institutional arrangements for the direct and indirect approach to warfare. The two debates need to be briefly addressed and distinguished, for they may remain on parallel tracks or converge in the future. First, regarding the direct and indirect approach, the argument has been made that units that specialize in the indirect approach play second fiddle to those specializing in direct action. The complaint was that those units had been shortchanged in resources because USSOCOM's leadership was drawn from direct action components. These leaders allegedly have been trying for decades to overcome the embarrassment of the Desert One failure by focusing on the direct action capabilities to the detriment of the indirect action units. Since the Army Special Forces are not only the largest component of USSOCOM but also the ones who work "by, with and through" indigenous forces, it should be no surprise that they were the main source of discontent.[424]

Two former civilian administrators in the DOD and DOS have been the main proponents for splitting USSOCOM into two four-star commands—one for direct action and another for indirect action forces.[425] They argued that a new indirect action command was needed to build up a new capability, a separate cadre of specialists on traditional networks. These would be Warrior diplomats trained in foreign languages and cultures who would serve about three tours of duty working and living abroad, immersing themselves in the local cultures. The Warrior diplomats would be key advisors if American forces need to deploy to their country or region; they would "serve as eyes and ears in places that U.S. and even local officials seldom visit … places where things of interest to the United States happen."[426] The leadership of USSOCOM and many SOF opposed the idea of creating a new command with separate leadership and budgets, however. As one former officer put it, "every time the secretary of defense says, 'I want to talk to my SOF guy,' two four-stars show up. It's an administrative and management nightmare."[427]

Admiral Olson responded to the idea by announcing that the USSOCOM mission to "deter, disrupt and defeat terrorist threats" was being advanced by turning USSOCOM's indirect action forces into "3D Operators." They would be career, multidimensional operators adept in the 3Ds.[428] He also spoke of Project Lawrence, along

...they would "serve as eyes and ears in places that U.S. and even local officials seldom visit...places where things of interest to the United States happen."

the model of Lawrence of Arabia, to find and train individuals with language skills, grounded in the local culture, diplomatically astute, and experts in specialized tactical skills.[429] The development of the indirect action units is a work in progress since in his last Posture Statement testimony as USSOCOM Commander, Admiral Olson noted that USSOCOM must "better understand the people and conditions in the places we go, whether to assist or fight."[430] One way to meet these needs is by recruiting qualified foreign-born residents who already meet the language and cultural qualifications who are incentivized to join the force by a process of accelerated citizenship status. One practical concern, of course, is that this recruitment pathway exposes the force to penetration by adversaries and must be met by a corresponding new emphasis on properly vetting the force and conducting counterintelligence. Admiral McRaven also believes in the use of indirect action.[431]

In the meantime, the push to make conventional forces more SOF-like was reinforced by Admiral Mullen's statement at a congressional hearing. As he put it, Admiral Olson's guidance for 2010 had struck him and Secretary Gates and, "I believe our whole military has to be looking at the kind of characteristics—swift, agile, lethal, engaging—all those kinds of things that are a part of our Special Forces as we look to the future for our conventional forces."[432] Movement along this track is driven not only by tighter budgets but also by the extant "new normal" interpretation of the current and future operational environment that guides prioritization of resources and capabilities.

The "new normal" global security environment is viewed as increasingly globalized, complex, and chaotic. Increased demand for natural resources, not solely oil, drives population movements and regional and global competition. Global communication, financial, and trading networks increase connectivity and interdependence of regional economies, cultures, and societies. During the Cold War, the security environment was more predictable and less complex because nation-states, and in particular the two superpowers, managed global friction and exerted control over information, which gave them primacy over their peoples.

The Westphalian state-system is being subjected to friction from trans-national crime, violent extremism, and migrations that compete with the nation-state for influence and access throughout the world. In essence, the nation-state system itself is challenged by super-national and non-state actors as internal domestic controls erode and sovereignty is contested or violated. An era of persistent conflict exists where individuals may identify less with the state and more with tribal groups, returning to ancestral territorial boundaries and familiar cultural norms. These factors are destabilizing and create opportunity for crime and extremism to flourish. Most of these trends are taking place in what Admiral Olson identified as the world's "unlit spaces" which have served as a point of reference for SOF missions since 2001.[433] The unlit spaces are mostly found in what geopolitical and social scientists call the global "South."

The Decisive Conventional Force Soldier and the SOF Operator

In the "new normal" global environment, the demand for more SOF is expected to increase to the point where they alone cannot respond in a timely manner without enabling support. One solution is to increase the number of SOF, but their highly selective entrance requirements has led to the belief that SOF-like units that do not meet the strict standards of recruitment, and selection might be just as effective. The Army, for instance, believes that in future conflicts it will continue to bear most of the casualties and the brunt of deployments, and therefore its dismounted soldiers, jumping from ground combat vehicles or dropping from Black Hawks, will need to operate in smaller units in hostile environments. To succeed, they would need to have "over-match" capability to fight the guys hiding behind the rocks. So the Army is searching to develop the soldier as a "decisive weapon."[434] According to Malcolm "Ross" O'Neill, Assistant Secretary of the Army for Acquisition, Logistics, and Technology, the new concepts include stealth and agility. The decisive dismounted soldier would be a technologically savvy operator who would be carrying something beyond a rifle, such as guided bullets or active sensors.[435]

The SOF-like dismounted soldier would work in small elements, bearing lighter loads in order to move quicker, and trained and equipped with more precise weapons in order to engage hostiles. Additionally, the small unit members would need better armor and have a greater capacity to communicate.[436] As explained by Lieutenant General Michael A. Vane, director of the Army Capabilities Integration Center and deputy commanding general for Futures at the U.S. Army TRADOC, decisive soldiers need to be physically and mentally tough, resilient, able to display strength of character and develop keen social skills to engage populations other than combatants, and develop respect for cultures other than their own. In sum, as he put it, "The direction we are headed in is to make our soldier more protected, connected and lethal on the battlefield."[437]

The Army emphasis on the decisive soldier as an adaptable field asset has led to the renewal of the debate over what makes SOF special. Major General Sacolick, a career special operations officer, for instance, endorsed the concept that America's conventional military forces, need to be more SOF-like. In his view, in a persistent conflict global environment, access is needed to troubled countries, as provided by the Obama administration policy of global engagement, or "the strategic use of development, diplomacy, and defense to advance our political agenda in areas like economic prosperity and international cooperation."[438] Sacolick's support for SOF-like expansion, however, is limited by his belief that the Army Special Forces, the Green Berets, are America's only trained Warrior diplomats, the only force we have that intuitively understands the balance between diplomacy and force, and the only force that possesses the judgment to determine which actions are most appropriate in any given situation. Special Forces soldiers understand that the key to success is through the indirect approach.[439] Hence, SOF-like conventional forces and SOF needed to be complementary.

The closing of the gap between SOF and conventional forces in operational capabilities compelled Michael G. Vickers, Under Secretary of Defense for Intelligence and the top DOD civilian advisor on CT strategy, to say that what makes SOF special is not necessarily "their tactical virtuosity and the skill of the individual operator," but rather it is their "strategic employment as a decisive instrument and their impact on the war that makes them special."[440] It is this focus on the strategic use of SOF that drives the current plan to build a global CT network focusing on "high priority" countries.[441]

In this context, the need to balance direct and indirect approaches is best understood by distinguishing between using SOF for strategic effects or strategic performance. As James Kiras explains, "The nature of special operations is derived from their conduct and character as they are unorthodox tactical actions for strategic effects that rely on exploiting an adversary's vulnerabilities to compensate for one's own small numbers."[442] Kiras associates achieving strategic effects with what USSOCOM describes as the direct approach. But strategic "effect" is not the same as strategic "performance." Strategic performance is:

> The cumulative effect of numerous disparate special operations, working toward a common goal in conjunction with conventional forces, is the attrition of an adversary's key moral and material resources. This psychological and physical erosion, combined with improving the strategic performance of one's own conventional forces, is how special operations contribute towards improving strategic performance. The challenge in special operations is to do the impossible not once but repeatedly.[443]

In other words, strategic performance is the result of repeated SOF direct action combined with an indirect approach to the enemy during an extended attrition-warfare campaign. In this sense, the best use of SOF for strategic performance is within an attrition-based strategy or interlinked series of engagements, rather than as an annihilation approach to warfare—annihilation meaning the attempt to eliminate the adversary by a "shock and awe," single, decisive engagement.[444] The key to success in the war against VEOs, therefore, requires a balanced approach in which SOF are used in an integrated and coherent strategy that deprives the enemy of "not only their leaders and key logistical elements, but also the moral hub that fuels recruitment and sustains the will to continue: their ideology."[445]

But direct actions may affect strategic performance. Thus, following the Osama bin Laden direct action operation, Secretary Gates opined, "I think that there's a possibility that it could be a game changer,"[446] meaning that it could lead to strategic performance. For example, cooperation in the war against terror became an organizing principle for Russian foreign policy with the United States, China, Europe, and India. The demise of bin Laden and the potential breakdown of al-Qaeda and its affiliates may change that landscape. Likewise, "If it brings about a change in Pakistani policies, then it would be a game changer," said Zalmay Khalilzad, the former U.S. ambassador to Afghanistan.[447]

Training SOF operators as Warrior diplomats for balanced warfare is not an easy task given the cultural differences and recruitment practices between DOD and DOS. The military is organized to wage war, while the diplomat is trained to employ peaceful means to advance the national interest and goals. Both sets of tasks ought to be complementary, but they become less so when performed by the same individual under combat conditions. As Anton Smith has noted, "The U.S. military, acting under plans in which everything is delineated in black and white fashion, generally follows orders. Diplomats, functioning in a zone where almost everything is gray, see themselves as interpreters of national policy."[448] Jessica Turnley compared the two roles in one aspect of the Warrior diplomat model by examining the competencies involved. One insight from her study was the "highly unequal distribution of cross-cultural competency across the special operations community."[449] But even if attainable, one should recall Henriksen's cautionary advice that the indirect approach has inherent limitations and must not be viewed as a one-size-fits-all solution to insurgency.[450]

Summary

Admiral McRaven confirmed Admiral Olson's views regarding USSOCOM's growth in force and the increased operational tempo issues. Congressional support is being sought for initiatives to increase "days at home" that would permit operators to spend more time with their families between deployments. One initiative seeks to diminish the "time away from home" factor by finding training facilities nearer to the operators' home stations. Lack of nearby training facilities means that operators need to "travel to train" away from home between deployments. It increases family and personal stress that could be remedied by either providing additional local facilities or allowing SOF priority access to existing local facilities. Land availability and environmental regulations are two obstacles that must be surmounted before SOF can build their own dedicated facilities.[451] Balanced warfare in an age of declining budgets remains a work in progress driven by facts on the ground, interagency collaborations issues, and conflicting theories of insurgency and COIN. Admiral Olson was absolutely right when he said it was difficult for SOF to balance the direct and indirect approaches when fighting a war of attrition. The balancing occurs not just among U.S. forces, capabilities, resources, interagency partners, and nongovernmental organizations, but also with indigenous partners and allies, as well as between competing perspectives on warfighting among the political and military elites. The success of the Osama bin Laden raid, however, might disprove the idea of short-lived effects of direct action. As previously noted, the possibility exists that the Osama bin Laden takedown achieved strategic performance. For example, if Afghanistan and Libya are "strategic distractions" from more critical concerns like the domestic economy, North Korea, a nuclear Iran, and the rise of China, then the bin Laden takedown will join the list of special operations, dating back to the Trojan Horse, that changed the destiny of nations.[452] While advocates of the indirect approach sing the praises of the good works being accomplished in Afghanistan, and others complain about turning the troops into "armed humanitarians" doing social work[453] or creating a "giant Peace Corps,"[454] the main questions remain unanswered. What is our grand strategy for the changing global order? What constitutes victory in 21st century warfare? General Petraeus understood the situation well years ago in Iraq when he asked *Washington Post* reporter Rick Atkinson the fundamental question of the Iraq war: "Tell me, how does this end?"[455]

5. Conclusion

> With good judgment, little else matters. Without it, nothing else matters. – N. Tichy and W. Bennis[456]

This study examined several themes associated with statecraft and power that bear on the roles and missions of SOF. There is no dominant theory that guides the policymaker in determining when and how to best use SOF as the military instrument of choice in pursuit of strategic ends. Absent of grand strategic vision linking means and ends, it becomes a judgment call based on ad hoc political considerations, ambiguous conceptualizations, or idiosyncratic interpretations of what constitutes the national interest, and/or how the world works or ought to work. Yet, there are times when military action is called for regardless of who happens to occupy the Oval Office. Franklin D. Roosevelt could not have gotten away with failing to declare war against Japan after Pearl Harbor. However, the daring Doolittle raid on Tokyo was great statecraft that lifted American morale. To this day, students of World War II debate why President Truman decided to authorize the bombing of Hiroshima—arguably the most important decision ever made. As the saying goes, you are where you sit. Instead of sending cruise missiles against abandoned buildings, why weren't SOF used by policymakers against al-Qaeda before the events of 9/11? Richard H. Shultz, Jr. listed nine "showstoppers" or self-imposed constraints that kept SOF from being used against the terrorists, ranging from treating terrorism as a crime, to risk aversion, to big footprints.[457] A different president might have chosen not to give the go ahead order when it came to the operation that killed Osama bin Laden. No matter what type of institutional process might be established, whether a Solarium type of exercise, muddling through, or a roll of the dice, in the U.S., when it comes to high politics decisions it all comes down to the judgment call of one person—the commander in chief, the president of the United States.

Leaders are remembered for their best and worst judgment calls. The same can be said about the individual SOF warrior sent on a risky mission where he is trusted to behave as trained, because the team's survival depends on his individual judgment and ability. It is at that point of the spear that the man in the Oval Office who gave the order and the operator executing it become one. Does judgment differ from common sense or gut instinct? Is it a product of luck or smarts? Is there a process for making consistent good calls? Tichy and Bennis studied how winning business leaders make great calls and identified the attributes of leaders who make successful judgments. Among them are: scanning the environment to find best practices, building good relationships, having character and courage to make a call based on values, measuring result of their judgment calls, and having the self-confidence to be wrong.[458]

In the political arena, those attributes of leadership may be fully present or partially absent among our policymakers. Americans tend to be pragmatic, not ideological people who elect pragmatic leaders regardless of political labels. Pragmatism, the living philosophy of the American people, might be one reason for the absence of a grand strategic vision. Nursed to be guided by practical experience and observation rather than theory, Americans appear culturally handicapped when strategizing for the long term.[459] But we must plan for an uncertain future. One should recall the impact of newly disclosed information every time historical records are unsealed or declassified. Most of the time they have led to major rewrites of history, as when the English double-cross system during World War II was revealed[460] or the Intrepid operation[461] or the Venona files.[462] In this digital age, perhaps people just sit and wait for the next batch of WikiLeaks.

The inability of civilian leaders to provide a grand organizing principle like the Cold War containment policy to guide us into an uncertain future has led to the belief that maybe our military leaders should provide those principles. But even the military appears to be afflicted by cultural limitations since, "The proper practice of strategy is the most significant challenge confronting senior leadership in the American military today."[463] One recent effort flowing from the ranks of the military is the recently proposed "A National Strategic Narrative" penned under the pseudonym of "Mr. Y" and published by the Woodrow Wilson Center at Princeton University.[464] The

> *The proper practice of strategy is the most significant challenge confronting senior leadership in the American military today.*

piece is not a household item, but it deserves close attention for several reasons. First, the preface is written by Anne-Marie Slaughter. As the DOS main strategist, she also co-directed the first QDDR. As previously noted, the

QDDR embodied the DOS's 21st century new statecraft and the administration's vision of the 3Ds. It is a commitment to a soft/smart power approach and sought authorities and funding to build the DOS expeditionary capacity that would help demilitarize American foreign policy.

Secondly, it was the DOD that released the report on 8 April 2011, and "Mr. Y" is the pseudonym for two military officers—Navy Captain Wayne Porter and Marine Colonel Mark "Puck" Mykleby—who served under Admiral Mullen, a supporter of soft power approaches. Third, the article ambitiously seeks to match Kennan's "Mr. X" article by attempting "to move beyond a strategy of containment to a strategy of sustainment ("sustainability"); from an emphasis on power and control to an emphasis on strength and influence; from a defensive posture of exclusion, to a proactive posture of engagement."[465]

Their narrative is grounded on Nye's soft power and smart power conceptualizations and echoes his recent complaint about a "war on soft power" as the United States goes through another round of "declinism."[466] It seeks to promote "smart growth" at home before exporting smart power abroad.[467] The authors believe that the U.S. reliance on the military for global engagement needs to change and propose a new 21st Century National Prosperity and Security Act along the lines of the National Security Act of 1947 and NSC-68. Undoubtedly, a direct connection exists between the timing and nature of the article: the reshuffling of President Obama's national security staff and the forthcoming budget cuts that threaten to derail the administration's 3Ds national security strategy announced by Secretary Clinton on 27 May 2010. Implementation of the QDDR is threatened by the fourth "D" of deficits that drive the budget cuts, in the amount of $8.5 billion, that Congress is set to impose on the DOS. Since both former Secretary Gates and Admiral Mullen supported increased funding and capacity for the DOS and USAID, the proposed new narrative reflects their thinking. It is one that, albeit supportive of the administration's foreign policy, seeks to refocus on our sources of strength while shrinking the defense budget to prevent an American collapse. So the study contains a not so subtle message to the Congress from the DOD itself that it should cut the defense, not the DOS and USAID budgets. The direct impact of the national deficits on foreign policy execution is already being felt, for instance, in the U.S. involvement in Libya where the U.S. was accused of leading from behind, and seeking multilateralism and/or burden sharing from our NATO partners and allies.

The issues and debates highlighted in this study suggest that SOF leadership must sustain a strong effort to convey to senior policymakers the message that SOF are a high-value, low-density asset with a high return on investment. In the absence of a grand strategy to guide policymakers, the SOF community should seek to develop and submit one for consideration. To have a continuous and sustained impact, the SOF community requires further integration into the national decision-making process so it can educate on its best use. SOF leadership should attempt to maintain direct access to senior policymakers to provide guidance on how to achieve strategic end goals while demonstrating that its special capabilities are not easily turned into modules for the entire military system. USSOCOM's accelerated growth in the last decade, albeit a welcome development, created an imbalance in relationship to other AORs as the force and resources were expanded and deployed as well as diverted from other areas to the CENTCOM AOR. This situation needs to be corrected as our global priorities change. Additionally, one question that needs to be addressed regarding growth is "growth to do what and to be where?"[468]

6. Epilogue, the Destruction of Troy— 1183 B.C.

The Greeks, after laying a fruitless 10-year siege to the city of Troy during the 12th century B.C. Trojan War, decided to hide *special forces* inside a huge and beautifully carved wooden horse.[469] It was a direct action operation with strategic impact that led to the fall of Troy and later to the founding of Rome by descendants of the surviving Trojan Prince Aeneas. The Greek leaders had approved a plan, drawn by Odysseus, the clever King of Ithaca, relying on deception, disinformation ("Beware of Greeks Bearing Gifts") and knowledge and understanding of the enemy, its culture, religious beliefs, and practices. It was a logistic feat that required the Greeks to embark their entire army and supplies on ships that would sail to a hiding place to await the attack signal. In those days, the politically correct thing to do after admitting defeat was to leave a gift. The Greeks decided to leave the Trojans the gift of a work of art. The 30 *special operators* inside the Wooden Horse were at high risk, and to achieve surprise had to move with speed, secrecy, under tight security, and with a clear purpose. It is unknown whether they rehearsed the operation, but it was a one-shot deal that had to be done with precision. The key to the success of the entire operation was one man, Simon, the *strategic communications special operator* left behind on the beach to perform the critical task of convincing the Trojans that the Greeks had indeed sailed away and the Trojans should take the horse into their city as a gift offering to their gods. Simon, the individual unit of action, could have been killed on the spot had the Trojans listened to the entreaties of the distrustful Laocoon and Cassandra. What might have been the fate of the men inside the horse? But the war weary and psychologically vulnerable Trojans were ready to believe Simon, particularly following the fateful sudden death of Laocoon. So believing they had won the war, the Trojans took the beautiful Wooden Horse into their high-walled city, partied well into the night, drinking themselves into a stupor—and the rest is history.♠

Endnotes

1. Samuel P. Huntington, "The Lonely Superpower: the new dimension of power," Foreign Affairs, March/April 1999, Vol. 78, #2, last accessed on 1/15/2011 at http://www.foreignaffairs.com/articles/54797/samuel-p-huntington/the-lonely-superpower.

2. On Russia see Peter Zeihan, "The Russian Resurgence and the New-Old Front," Geopolitical Weekly, Stratfor, Monday, September 15, 2008. Fareed Zakaria, "The Rise of the Rest," Newsweek, May 3, 2008; accessible at http://www.newsweek.com/2008/05/03/the-rise-of-the-rest.html.

3. "Putting 'Smart Power' to Work: The Report on Reports," Center for U.S. Global Engagement, Washington, DC, March 4, 2009; accessible at www.usglc.org/2009/03/04/putting-smart-power-to-work-report-release.

4. Paul Joseph Watson, "Report: US Special Forces Arrive in Libya," Infowars.com, March 1, 2011; accessible at www.infowars.com/report-us-special-forces-arrive-in-libya.

5. "China As No. 1? Give us a Break," Investor's Business Daily, 25 April 2011, p. 1. See also "Davos elites see global economic shift East, South," Breibart.com, January 26, 2011, http://www.breitbart.com/article.php?id=CNG.beec3d7690e-44a9b7cb55c470f8c4b.181&show_article=1 (last accessed on 1/27/11); and Jonathan Holslag, "Trapped Giant: China's Military Rise," The International Institute for Strategic Studies, New York: Routledge, 2010.

6. Paul Kennedy, The Rise and Fall of Great Power, New York, Random House, 1987. For a critical review of declinism see Alan W. Dowd, "Declinism," Policy Review, No. 144, August 1, 2007; accessible at www.hoover.org/publications/policy-review/article/5864; for an anti-declinist view see Henry N. Nau, The Myth of America's Decline, New York, Oxford University Press, 1991.

7. Joseph S. Nye, Jr., Bound to Lead: The Changing Nature of American Power, New York, Basic Books, Inc., 1990; Paul Kennedy, The Rise and Fall of Great Power, New York, Random House, 1987.

8. Osama Bin Laden, "Declaration of Jihad Against the Americans Occupying the Land of the Two Holiest Sites," 1996, translated by Counter Terrorism Center (CTC) at West Point Military Academy; accessible at http://en.wikisource.org/wiki/Osama_bin_Laden's_Declaration_of_War (last accessed on October 23, 2010).

9. Wan Guang, Meiguo de shehui bing (American Social Diseases) Chengdu: Sichuan renmin chubanshe, 1997, pp. 1-5 in Michael Pillsbury, China Debates the Future Security Environment, Washington, DC, NDU Press, 2000, pp. 87-88.

10. Jeff Gannon, "Clinton Predicts America's Decline," Talon News, May 5, 2003; last accessed on 1/26/11 at <http://mensnewsdaily.com/archive/newswire/nw03/talonnews/0503/newswire-tn-050503d.htm> Clinton himself has been severely criticized for contributing to China's military ascent. His open-door foreign policy promoting "multipolarity" allowed defense contractors to sell China

technology that helped modernize its nuclear strike force. Ron Brown, Clinton's secretary of commerce and the alleged contact with the Chinese, was under investigation for corruption when he died in a mysterious 1996 plane crash in Croatia. Clinton allegedly helped China by appointing as head of the Department of Energy anti-nuclear activist Hazel O'Leary who favored "leveling the playing field" by declassifying millions of pages with data on U.S. nuclear weapons. Under her leadership, security at American weapons labs was loosened as revealed by the Wen Ho Lee nuclear espionage case. For more see, "Report of the Select Committee on U.S. National Security and Military/Commercial Concerns with the People's Republic of China" (The Cox Report) redacted, declassified version, U.S. House of Representatives, May 25, 1999, accessible at <http://www.house.gov/ coxreport/> See Steve Wampler, "The Johnny Chung story," Infowars, accessible at <http://www.infowars.com/jchung.html>; Richard Pope, "The Idiot's Guide to Chinagate," <www.richardpoe.com/column.cgi?story=125>.

11. Gideon Rachman, "Think Again: American Decline: This time it is for real," Foreign Policy, January/February, 2011 pp. 59-63.

12. Joseph P. Nye, Jr. "The Future of American Power," Foreign Affairs, November/December 2010, Vol. 89. No. 6, pp. 2-12.

13. Jonah Goldberg, "America's China Syndrome," Los Angeles Times, Jan. 19, 2011, accessible at www.latimes.com/news/opinion/commentary/la-oe-goldberghu-20110118,0,1017628.column.

14. This argument is advanced by none other than Paul Kennedy who originated the debate on decline. See Paul Kennedy, "Back to Normalcy: Is America really in decline?" The New Republic, December 21, 2010, last accessed on 1/27/11 at http://www.tnr.com/article/magazine/79753/normalcy-american-decline-decadence.

15. Fareed Zakaria, The Post-American World, New York: W.W. Norton & Co., 2009.

16. See, for instance, William C. Wohlforth, "Shifting from a Unipolar to a Multipolar World?" Rethinking US Grand Strategy and Foreign Policy Seminar Series, 21 January 2010, accessible at https://outerdnn.outer.jhuapl.edu/videos/012110/wohlforth.pdf.

17. See National Intelligence Council, Global Trends 2025: A World Transformed, Washington, DC, NIC, November 2008 www.dni.gov/nic/NIC_2025_project.html.

18. William J. Antholis and Martin Indyk, "How We're Doing Compared to the Rest of the World," Washington: DC, The Brookings Institution, February 15, 2011, accessible at http://www.brookings.edu/papers/2011/0213_recovery_renewal.aspx?p=1.

19. Dale Jorgenson as quoted in Mark Felsenthal, "Economists foretell of U.S. decline, China's ascension." Reuters, 9 Jan, 2011; available at http//www.reuters.com/assets/print?aid=USTRE7082BL20110109.

20. "Admiral Mike Mullen: "National Debt is Our Biggest Security Threat'," Huffington Post, 25 June, 2010; accessible at http://politifi.com/news/Adm-Mike-Mullen-National-Debt-Is-Our-Biggest-Security-Threat-858639.html.

21. Walter Alarkon, "Clinton says deficit is national security threat," The Hill, September 8, 2010; accessible at http://thehill.com/blogs/on-the-money/budget/117723-clinton-us-deficit-sends-qmessage-of-weakness-internationallyq.

22. United States Department of the Treasury, Bureau of the Public Debt, "The debt to the penny and who holds it." TreasuryDirect, December 2010. Retrieved on March 2, 2011 from http://www.treasurydirect.gov/NP/BPDLogin?application=np.

23. Fred Kaplan, "The Transformer" Foreign Policy, Sept/Oct. 2010 accessed on December 20, 2011 at www.foreignpolicy.con/articles/2010/08/16/the_transformer.

24. Larry J. Korb, "Alarmist Defense Cuts Won't Help the Deficit," Center for American Progress, accessed on 8/10/10 www.americanprogress.org/issues/2010/08/gates_announcement.html.

25. Arthur Herman, "The Re-Hollowing of the Military," Commentary, September 2010 accessed on 8/12/10 at www.commentarymagazine.com/viewarticle.cfm/the-re-hollowing-of-the-military-15498.

26. The budget to finance the Iraq and Afghanistan wars is separate from the DOD operating budget. Nathan Hodge and Julian E. Barnes, "Pentagon Faces the Knife," Wall Street Journal, Friday, 1/7/2011, p. A1. See also, Thom Shanker and Christopher Drew, "Pentagon Seeks Biggest Military Cuts Since Before 9/11," The New York Times, January 6, 2011.

27. See, "The FY2012 Defense Budget: What to Expect in an Age of Austerity," CSBA Backgrounder, Washington: DC, February 10, 2011.

28. John T. Bennett, "Armed Services chairman has 'significant concerns' about DOD budget plan," The Hill, February 14, 2011 accessed on February 16 at http://thehill.com/homenews/administration/143903-gates-pentagons-671b-budget-plan-reasonable-responsible.

29. Quote from Loren Thompson. Ibid.

30. Thomas P. M. Barnett, "The New Rules" U.S. Defense Cuts a Step in the Right Direction," World Politics Review, January 10, 2011; accessible at http://www.worldpoliticsreview.com/articles/7502/the-new-rules-u-s-defense-cuts-a-step-in-the-right-direction.

31. Jonathan Berr, "U.S. Defense Cuts Present A Huge Opportunity For The Chinese," 24/7 Wall St. January 19, 2011 accessible at http://247wallst.com/2011/01/19/u-s-defense-cuts-present-a-huge-opportunity-for-the-chinese/.

32. Gordon Adams and Matthew Leatherman, "A Leaner and Meaner Defense, Foreign Affairs, Vol. 90, No. 1, Jan/Feb 2011, pp. 139-152.

33. Joint Force Command cuts 2,300 in Virginia; MacDill will lose jobs," The Associated Press, 9 February, 2011 <www2.tbo.com/content/2011/feb/09/092238/closing-of-joint-force-command-to-cut-2300-jobs-in/>.

34. The White House, "Remarks by the President on Fiscal Policy," George Washington University, Washington, DC, April 13, 2011 Accessible at www.whitehouse.gov/the-press-office/2011/04/13/remarks--president-fiscal-policy.

35. Robert M. Gates, "A Balanced U.S. Military Strategy," Foreign Affairs, Vol. 88, No. 1, January/February 2009, pp. 28-40.

36. The National Military Strategy of the United States (NMS) is a deliverable from the Chairman of the Joint Chiefs of Staff to the Secretary of Defense briefly outlining the strategic aims of the armed services. The NMS's chief source of guidance is the National Security Strategy document. See, 2011 National Military Strategy, 8 February 2011; www.defense.org.

37. See James R. Clapper, DNI "Unclassified Statement for the Record on the World-wide Threat Assessment of the US Intelligence community for the Senate Select Committee on Intelligence," Statement for the Record, Senate Select Committee on Intelligence, Washington, DC, January 31, 2012. Last accessed February 14, 2012 at http://www.dni.gov/testimonies/20120202_testimony_wta.pdf.

38. Thucydides, The Peloponnesian War, New York: E. P. Dutton. 1910, Book 1, Chapter 76, Section 2.

39. Carl Philipp Gottfried von Clausewitz, Vom Kriege (On War) edited and translated by Michael Howard and Peter Paret, Princeton: Princeton University Press, revised 1984, pp. 69-70.

40. John G. Stoessinger, Why Nations Go To War, 11th. Ed., Lexington: KY, Cengage Learning, Inc. 2010.

41. J. David Singer, "The Levels of Analysis Problem in International Relations," World Politics, Vol. 14, No.1, The International System Theoretical Essays, October 1961, pp. 77-92.

42. "McChrystal Speaks on Leadership and Composites," ACMA, press release, February 3, 2011; www.acmanet.org.

43. Robert Jervis, Ole Holsti, David Sears, and M. Brewster Smith, "Political Psychology—Challenges and Opportunities," Political Psychology 10 (1989) pp. 481-516; Robert Jervis, Perception and Misperception in International Relations, Princeton: New Jersey, Princeton University Press, 1976.

44. John F. Kennedy, "Remarks at Annapolis to the Graduating Class of the United States Naval Academy," 7 June 1961, John T. Woolley and Gerhard Peters, The American Presidency Project (Santa Barbara: University of California, Santa Barbara); accessible at http://www.presidency.ucsb.edu/ws/pid=8181.

45. See Robert Spulak's recommendation of a "rapid innovation braid" in his Innovate or Die: Innovation and Technology for Special Operations, JSOU Report 10-7, JSOU Press, MacDill Air Force Base, Florida, 2010.

46. The other truths are: quality is better than quantity, competent SOF cannot be created after emergencies occur, and most special operations require non-SOF support. Fact Book, United States Special Operations Command, USSOCOM Public Affairs, pp. 44-45.

47. David Tucker and Christopher J. Lamb, "Restructuring Special Operations Forces for Emerging Threats," Strategic Forum, Institute for National Strategic Studies, National Defense University, No. 219, January 2005, p. 1.

48. *Grand Strategies: Literature, Statecraft, and World Order*, Yale, 2010.

49. David A. Baldwin, *Economic Statecraft*, Princeton, NJ: Princeton University Press, 1985, p. 8.

50. A. Codevilla, op. cit., p. 1.

51. Chas. W. Freeman, Jr., *Arts of Power: Statecraft and Diplomacy*, Washington, DC, United States Institute of Peace Press, 1997, pp. 3-5, 123.

52. Jessica Glicken Turnley, *Cross-Cultural Competence and Small Groups: Why SOF are the way SOF are*, JSOU Report 11-1, JSOU Press, 2011, p. 9.

53. The International Raoul Wallenberg Foundation, lists over 75 savior diplomats. See http://www.raoulwallenberg.net/news/ceremony-honoring-mexican/. Last accessed on November 15, 2010.

54. Freeman, op. cit., pp. 45-52.

55. Dennis Ross, *Statecraft and How to Restore America's Standing in the World*, New York, Farrar, Straus and Giroux, 2007, p. 21.

56. Ibid., 23.

57. Freeman, op. cit.

58. M. Kaplan, op. cit., p. 548.

59. Hill, Grand Strategies, op. cit., p. 178.

60. A. J. P. Taylor, *The Struggle for Mastery in Europe, 1848-1918*, Oxford, UK: Oxford University Press, 1954, xxix.

61. "How Many Divisions Does the Pope Have," Voices From Russia, 10 December 2009; last accessed on January15 at <http://02varvara.wordpress.com/2009/12/10/how-many-divisions-does-the-pope-of-rome-have/?>.

62. Kurt M. Campbell and Michael E. O'Hanlon, *Hard Power: The New Politics of National Security*, New York: Basic Books, 2006, Robert Cooper, " The Goals of Diplomacy, Hard Power, Soft Power," David Held, Mathias Koenig-Archibugi (eds) American Power in the 21ST Century, Cambridge: Polity, John Wiley & Sons, 2004, pp. 167-180.

63. Otto von Bismarck (1815-98) Speech in the Prussian House of Deputies, 28 January 1886. Famous Quotes; last accessed on 12 February 2011 at <http://mr_sedivy.tripod.com/quotes10.html>; In an earlier speech, on 30 September 1862, Bismarck used the form 'iron and blood.'

64. Joseph S. Nye Jr., *Bound to Lead: The Changing Nature of American Power*, New York: Basic Books, 1990.

65. Joseph S. Nye, Jr." Think Again: Soft Power," Foreign Policy, February 23, 2006 http://www.foreignpolicy.com/articles/2006/02/22/think_again_soft_power (last accessed on January 29, 2011).

66. Joseph Nye, Jr. "Smart Power: In Search of the balance between hard and soft power," Democracy: a Journal of Ideas, Issue 2, Fall 2006, pp. 102-107.

67. Huntington, op. cit., pp. 92-93.

68. Joseph P. Nye, Jr., "Soft Power and Leadership," Compass: A Journal of Leadership, Spring 2004 reproduced as "The Benefits of Soft Power," on 8/2/2004 at http://hbswk.hbs.edu/archive/4290.html. Nye first made the point that the distinction between hard and soft power resources was one of degree in a footnote in his 1990 book Bound to Lead, op. cit., p.267.

69. "Transcript of Bin Laden Videotape", NPR, December 13, 2011, http://www.npr.org/news/specials/response/investigation/011213.binladen.transcript.html.

70. Nye, Think Again, op. cit.

71. Robert Conquest, The Great Terror: Stalin's Purge of the Thirties (1968) A revised version of the book, called The Great Terror: A Reassessment, Oxford University Press, was printed in 1990 after Conquest was able to amend the text, having consulted recently opened Soviet archives.

72. On the Committees of Correspondence see "Committees of Correspondence," Boston Tea Party Ships and Museum, Historic Tours of America at www.bostonteapartyship.com/committees-of-correspondence. On Paul Revere see Facts on Paul Revere-Revolutionary War and Beyond, "Did he see military action during the war" at www.revolutionary-war-and-beyond.com/facts-on-paul-revere.html. "Paul Revere's Ride: The Patriots Prepare for Battle, at www.bostonteapartyship.com/paul-reveres-ride; Paul Revere Heritage Project, "Paul Revere's Midnight Ride", www.paul-revere-heritage.com/midnight-ride.html.

73. Ibid.

74. George Creel, Advertising America: The First Telling of the Amazing Story of the Committee on Public Information that Carried the Gospel of Americanism to Every Corner of the World, New York: Harper & Brothers, 1920, p. 4.

75. Ted J. Smith, "Social Responses to Twentieth-Century Propaganda," in Ted J. Smith ed. Propaganda, New York: Praeger, p. 8.

76. Daniel H. Nexon, "The Balance of Power in the Balance," World Politics, Vol. 61, No. 2, April 2009, p. 343 fn. 37.

77. Eric Schwartz, "How Can We Know How Well Soft-Power Works? Some thought on Empirical Testing and A Preliminary Test," Paper presented at the annual meeting of the APSA, August 30, 2007; http://allacademic.com/meta/p210057_index.html (last accessed on April 12, 2011).

78. FM 3-07, Foreword, Stability Operations, 6 October 2008, Washington, DC, HQ Department of the Army. Available at www.us.army.mil.

79. Robert M. Gates, U.S. Secretary of Defense, "Landon Lecture: Remarks as Delivered by Secretary of Defense Robert M. Gates," transcript of address at Kansas State University, November 26, 2007.

80. U.S. Secretary of Defense, Robert M. Gates speech at National Defense University, U. S. Department of Defense, Washington, DC, Monday, September 29, 2008 http://www.defense.gov/Speeches/Speech.aspx?SpeechID=127. Last accessed on January 19, 2011.

81. "Green Berets", John F. Kennedy Presidential Library and Museum, http://www. jfklibrary.org/JFK/JFK-in-History/Green-Berets.aspx.

82. "Peace Corps," John F. Kennedy Presidential Library, and Museum; accessed on February 1, 2011 at http://www.jfklibrary.org/JFK/JFK-in-History/Peace-Corps. aspx; see also "Alliance for Progress and Peace Corps," Department of State at http:// future.state.gov/when/timeline/1946_cold_war_progress_and_peace_ corps.html.

83. www.southcom.mil/appssc/factFiles.php?id=155.

84. "Europe's Agenda 2000: Strengthening and Widening the European Union," Draft of Commission information brochure for the general public on Agenda 2000, Priority Publications Programme 1999, X/D/5, final version 31.8. ENI 25.10.

85. Robert Cooper, "Hard Power, Soft Power and the Goals of Diplomacy," in David Held, Mathias Koenig-Archibugi (eds), *American Power in the 21st Century*, 2004, pp. 167-180.

86. Qatar Travel, http://www.traveleguides.com/qatar.php.

87. Carl Ungerer, "The 'Middle Power' Concept in Australian Foreign Policy," The Journal of Politics and History, 2007, Vol. 53, No. 4, p. 548.

88. David Pollock, "Aljazeera: One Organization, Two Messages," PolicyWatch #1802, April 28, 2011; accessible at http://washingtoninstitute.org/templateC05. php?CID=3355.

89. http://en.wikipedia.org/wiki/Doha_Agreement.

90. The four planes were blown off course, nearly ran out of fuel after being refused landing rights by Cyprus, and almost ditched on the sea before declaring a fuel emergency and landing on the Greek island of Crete. See news report at http://www. ihatethemedia.com/qatari-air-force-runs-out-of-fuel-almost-has-to-ditch-in-sea.

91. "Hu Jintao calls for enhancing 'soft power of Chinese culture," October 15, 2007, Beijing: People's Daily; accessible at htpp://english.peopledaily.com. cn/90002/92187/6283148.html (last accessed on February 2, 2011).

92. Josh Kurlantzick, *Charm Offensive: How China's Soft Power is Transforming the World*, New Haven: Conn, Yale University Press, 2007.

93. Peter Mattis, "Reexamining the Confucian Institutes", *The Diplomat*, August 2, 2012, at thediplomat.com/china-power/reexamining-the-confucian-institutes/; see also, "Confucius Institutes Around the Globe" at www.confuciusinstitute. unl.edu/institutes.shtml.

94. www.cfr.org/publications/10715/ chinas_soft_power_initiative.html#p3.

95. Arthur Waldron, ed., *China in Africa*, Washington: DC, Jamestown Foundation, September, 2008.

96. R. Evan Ellis, "Chinese Soft Power in Latin America: a Case Study," Joint Force Quarterly, NDU Press, Issue 60, 1st Quarter 2011, p. 86.

97. Ibid., 86-87.

98. Ibid., 90-91.

99. See Video: "World Insight 11/02/06 China's image abroad" at http://english.cntv. cn/program/worldinsight/20110210/105953.shtml.

100. Susan Brownell, "China's National Image in the Beijing Olympics and Shanghai Expo," China's Soft Power in the Making: Mega Events, Governance, and Peaceful Rise in Chinese Politics--Roundtable on China's Soft Power, UCLA Center for Chinese Studies, January 27, 2011.

101. Beijing's Buildup Stirs Fears," The Wall Street Journal, March 5/6, 2011, p. A10.

102. Markus Wolf, *Man Without a Face*, New York: Public Affairs, 1997, Chapter 15.

103. State of Terrorism, Office of the Coordinator for Counterterrorism, Country Reports on Terrorism 2011, U.S. Department of State, Country Reports on Terrorism 2011 , accessible at http://www.state.gov/j/ct/rls/crt/2011/195547.htm. See also Pamela Falk "Cuba in Africa", *Foreign Affairs*, Summer 1987, http://www. foreignaffairs.com/articles/42294/pamela-s-falk/cuba-in-africa; "Cuban Intervention in Angola", *Wikipedia*, https://en.wikipedia.org/wiki/Cuban_intervention_in_Angola; "Cuba's Renewed Support of Violence in Latin America," U.S. Department of State, Bureau of Public Affairs, December 14, 1981.

104. Ibid., See also Robert M. Morgenthau, "Morgenthau: The Link Between Iran and Venezuela -- A Crisis in the Making?" Brookings Institution, Washington, DC , September 8, 2009. Also reported in the Latin American Herald Tribune at http://laht.com/article.asp?ArticleId=343289&CategoryId=10718; "Castro and Terrorism: A Chronology", Staff Report, ICCAS, Issue 57, July 29, 2004, Miami, FL.

105. See Louis Perez Jr., Cuba: *Between Reform and Revolution*, New York: NY, Oxford University Press, 1988, pp.377-379; John Hoyt Williams, "Cuba: Havana's Military Machine," *The Atlantic*, August 1, 1988 at www.theatlantic.com/magazine/archive/1988/08/cuba-havana.

106. There is a voluminous literature on the Cuban Revolution and Fidel Castro. A recent contribution that adds new value are: Daniel P. Erikson, *The Cuba Wars: Fidel Castro, the United States and the Next Revolution*, New York: Bloomsbury Press, 2008. See also, Georgie Anne Geyer, Guerrilla Prince: The Untold Story of Fidel Castro, Boston: Little Brown and Co., 1991; Hugh Thomas, Cuba or the Pursuit of Freedom, updated edition, New York: De Capo Press, 1998.

107. Daniel P. Erikson, *The Cuba Wars: Fidel Castro, the United States and the Next Revolution*, New York: Bloomsbury Press, 2008. See also: Michael Casey, *Che's Afterlife: The Legacy of an Image*, New York: Random House, 2009.

108. Jaime Suchlicki, *Cuba: From Columbus to Castro and Beyond*, 5th ed. Washington, DC: Brassey's Inc., 2002.

109. Julie M. Feinsilver, "Fifty Years of Cuba's Medical Diplomacy: From Idealism to Pragmatism," Cuban Studies, Volume 41, 2010, pp. 85-104.

110. http://en.wikipedia.org/wiki/The_Motorcycle_Diaries_ percent28film percent29.

111. One of the most influential self-help books to influence the world over is Dale Carnegie's, *How to Make Friends and Influence People*, originally published in 1937 by New York's Simon & Schuster.

112. "The Elian Gonzalez Case," The Washington Post last accessed on January 30, 2011 at http://www.washingtonpost.com/wp-dyn/nation/specials/aroundthe-nation/elian/; see also "The Elian Gonzalez case," Special Report, Guardian News & Media, accessible at http://www.guardian.co.uk/elian.

113. See list of references in footnote vii in Matthew Kroenig, Melissa McAdam, and Steven Weber "Taking Soft Power Seriously"; accessible at www.matthewkroenig.com/Kroenig_Taking_Soft_Power_Seriously.pdf. Later published as Matthew Kroenig, Melissa McAdam and Steven Weber, "Taking Soft Power Seriously," Comparative Strategy, Vol. 29, Issue 5, 2010, pp. 412-431.

114. Remarks by the President "On a New Beginning," Cairo University, Cairo, Egypt, June 4, 2009; last accessed on December 15, 2010 at http://www.whitehouse.gov/the-press-office/remarks-president-cairo-university-6-04-09.

115. Kroenig et. al. Taking Soft Power Seriously, op. cit.

116. Ibid., 414-425.

117. U.S. Army TRADOC, "Joint Low-Intensity Conflict Project Final Report.," Analytical Review of Low-Intensity Conflict, Vol. 1, 1986.

118. Department of the Army, Counterinsurgency Field Manual No. 3-24, December 2006; accessible at http://www.fas.org/irp/doddir/army/fm3-24.pdf.

119. Kroenig op. cit.

120. Seymour M. Hersch, "Torture at Abu Ghraib," The New Yorker, May 10, 2004; http//www.newyorker.com/archive/2004/05/10/040510fa_fact (accessed on January 31, 2011).

121. Donald Rumsfeld, *Known and Unknown*: A Memoir, New York: Penguin Group, 2011.

122. Amy Chua, *World on Fire: How Exporting Free Market Democracy Breeds Ethnic Hatred and Global Instability*, New York: Doubleday, 2002.

123. David C. Hendrickson and Robert W. Tucker, *Revisions in Need of Revising: What Went Wrong in the Iraq War?* Carlisle: PA: Strategic Studies Institute-U.S. Army War College, December 2005.

124. Robert T. Hastings, "Principles of Strategic Communication," US Department of Defense, 15 August, 2008. See also, "What is Strategic Communication?," Comment by Grim, Mountainrunner, December 15, 2009; accessed on February 1, 2011 at http://mountainrunner.us/2009/12/whatissc.html#comment-5196. Strategic communications (SC) is being replaced by "communications synchronization" in the DOD lexicon per OASD Memorandum for Commanders of the Combatant Command, dated 28 November 2012. SC is used here because of its relevance to the earlier study.

125. Kroenig, op. cit., pp. 29-30.

126. Ibid.

127. Ibid., 28-29. See also by point of comparison Secretary Gates 2008 speech at NDU, op. cit.

128. Suzanne Nossel, "Smart Power," Foreign Affairs, March/April 2004, Vol. 83, No. 2, pp. 131-143.

129. Ibid., 134.

130. Ibid., 134-35.

131. Ibid., 138.

132. Ibid., 136-42.

133. Joseph P. Nye, "Get Smart-Combining Hard and Soft Power," Foreign Affairs, July/ August 2009 accessible at www.foreignaffairs.com/articles/65163/joseph-s-nye-jr/ get-smart.

134. Suzanne Nossel, "Hard Power/Soft Power/Smart Power," 29 October, 2006, www. democracyarsenal.org/2006/10/smart_power_a_p.html.

135. Eric Etheridge, "How 'Soft Power' Got Smart," Opinionator, The New York Times, 14 January, 2009; accessible at <http://opinionator.blogs.nytimes.com/2009/01/14/ how-soft-power-got-smart/>.

136. http://csis.org/publication/smarter-more-secure-america.

137. Ibid.

138. "CSIS Commission on Smart Power—A Smarter, More Secure America," CSIS, Washington, DC, 2007, pp. 27-60; last accessed on April 25, 2011 at http://csis. org/files/media/csis/pubs/071106_csissmartpowerreport.pdf.

139. Ibid, 1.

140. Coit D. Blacker, "Director's Letter," in The New Global Agenda: Tackling Poverty, Bridging Divides, Building Institutions, Annual Report 2010,Freeman Spogli Institute for International Studies, Palo Alto, CA, Stanford University, p. 3.

141. Gates, Landon Lecture, op. cit.

142. Hillary Rodham Clinton, Statement before the Senate Foreign Relations Committee, Washington, DC, January 13, 2009; accessible at http://www.state.gov/ secretary/rm/2009a/01/115196.htm.

143. U.S. Department of State, Leading Through Civilian Power: 2010 Quadrennial Diplomacy and Development Review, Washington, DC; Global Publishing Solutions, 2010, Executive Summary, p. 8.

144. http://www.state.gov/r/pa/scp/fs/2009/122579.htm.

145. www.mitre.org/tech.smartpower.

146. Derek Henry Flood, Jamestown Foundation Conference on Middle East and Africa, Washington, DC, Wednesday, April 20, 2011.

147. Dina Shehata, "The Fall of the Pharaoh: How Hosni Mubarak's reign came to an end," Foreign Affairs, Vol. 90, No 2, May/June, 2011 p. 28.

148. James Cowie, "Egypt Leaves the Internet" January 27, 2011, Renesys Blog, accessed on Feb. 19, 2011 at http://www.renesys.com/blog/2011/01/egypt-leaves-the-internet.shtml.

149. Matt Richtel, "Egypt Cuts Off Most Internet and Cell Service," The New York Times, January 28, 2011; last accessed on Feb. 19, 2011 at http://www.nytimes.com/2011/01/29/technology/internet/29cutoff.html.

150. Joe Gandelman, "Obama Tells Egypt's Beset Mubarak That He Must Keep His Promises," The Moderate Voice, January 28, 2011, accessed on 2/19/11 at http://themoderatevoice.com/99639/obama-tells-egypts-beset-mubarak-that-he-must-keep-his-promises/.

151. Alana Silverleib, "Bahrain: What's at Stake for America," CNN, February 17, 2011 accessed at http://articles.cnn.com/2011-02-17/us/us.bahrain.stakes_1_isa-al-khalifa-bahrainis-king-hamad?_s=PM:US.

152. Christina Shelton, "The Roots of Analytic Failures in the U.S. Intelligence Community," International Journal of Intelligence and Counterintelligence, 24: 6237:655, 2011.

153. For a claim that we missed the Arab revolts due to old fashioned American stupidity see M.G. Piety, "Why the U.S. Didn't Foresee the Arab Revolts?—The Writing on the Wall," February 28, 2011; accessible at http://markganzersblog.blogspot.com/2011/02/why-us-didnt-foresee-arab-revolts.html.

154. Bradley Klapper, Associated Press, Star Tribune, Minneapolis-St Paul, MN, 25 January 2011. "Quick Facts: US Flip-flop on Egypt," Press TV, Saturday February 5, 2011; accessible at http://www.presstv.ir/usdetail/163816.html.

155. Fred Kaplan, "Mubarak's Bombshell," Slate, February 10, 2011, accessible at http://www.slate.com/id/2284669/.

156. Jonathan Broder," Lawmakers Concerned About Egypt," Congress.org, February 2, 2011; accessible at http://www.congress.org/news/2011/02/11/lawmakers_concerned_about_egypt.

157. Nancy A Youssef. Jonathan S. Landay, Warren P. Strobe, "Khadafy pressed to stop violence," San Francisco Chronicle, March 1, 2011, p. A3.

158. "Top Sunni cleric says army should kill Kadhafi" Feb. 21, 2011; access at http://news.yahoo.com/s/afp/20110221/wl_mideast_afp/libyapoliticsunrestfatwa_20110221212046.

159. "Some of the Key Events in Moammar Gaddafi's Rule," Los Angeles Times, Sept. 4, 2005; accessible at www.latimes.com/news/printedition/la-fg-uslibyachrono4sep04,0,2259746.

160. Steven Emerson and Brian Duffy, The Fall of Pan Am 103: Inside the Lockerbie Investigation, New York: Putnam, 1990; Karla Adam, "Man Convicted In Lockerbie Blast Is Freed," The Washington Post, August 21, 2009; accessed on 30 August 2011 at http://www.washingtonpost.com/wpdyn/content/article/2009/08/20/AR2009082000545.Html.

161. http://www.state.gov/secretary/rm/2009a/july/126071.htm.

162. Secretary of State Hillary Clinton "Remarks on Internet Freedom," The Newseum, January 21, 2010; accessible at http://www.state.gov/secretary/rm/2010/01/135519.htm.

163. Ibid.

164. Alec Ross, "21st Century Statecraft Background," January 20, 2010 at http://www.state.gov/statecraft/rm/135545.htm.

165. Secretary Clinton's Speech on Internet Freedom, Real Clear Politics, February 15, 2011; accessible at http://www.reealclearpolitics.com/articles/2011/02/15/secretary_clintons_speech_on_internet_freedom_108920.html.

166. Ibid. (See also David Leigh and Luke Harding, *WikiLeaks: Inside Julian Assange's War on Secrecy*, New York: Public Affairs, 2011).

167. Clinton's Speech on Internet Freedom, op. cit.

168. Mary Beth Sheridan and Scott Wilson, "U.S. struggles with little leverage to restrain Libyan government," The Washington Post, Tuesday, February 22, 2011; accessible at www.washingtonpost.com/wpdyn/content/article/2011/02/21/AR2011022105003.html?nav=rss_email/components&sid=ST2011022105046.

169. Ibid.

170. "Obama says U.S. readying full range of options on Libya," Reuters, February 23, 2011; accessible at http://www.reuters.com/article/2011/02/23/us-libya-usa-obama-statement-idUSTRE71M76T20110223.

171. Nancy A Youssef, Jonathan S. Landay, Warren P. Strobe, "Gaddafi pressed to stop violence," San Francisco Chronicle, March 1, 2011, p. A3.

172. Ibid.

173. See for instance, Helene Cooper and Steven Lee Myers, "Obama Takes Hard Line With Libya After Shift by Clinton," The New York Times, March 18, 2011; also Josh Rogin, "How Obama Turned on a Dime Toward War," Foreign Policy, March 18, 2011 accessible at http://thecable.foreignpolicy.com/posts/2011/03/18/how_obama_turned_on_a_dime_toward_war.

174. Andrew Young Presents, "Rwanda Rising," Andrew Young Foundation, 8 February, 2007; accessible at OperationHope.org.

175. UN Department of Public Information, New York, 17 March, 2011 http://www.un.org/News/Press/docs/2011/sc10200.doc.htm.

176. Thomas Risse, "Democratic Peace—Warlike Democracies; A Social Constructivist Interpretation of the Liberal Argument," European Journal of International Relations, Vol. 1, (1995), No. 4, pp. 491-518.

177. Robert M. Gates, "A Balanced Strategy," op. cit., p. 39.

178. Elmer Plischke, *Foreign Relations: Analysis of Its Anatomy*, New York: Greenwood Press, 1988, p.54. See also Christopher D. Carey, "The Changing Nature of Credibility: From Interest to Instrument to Vital Interest, or How I Learned to Stop Worrying and Love "The Box," Washington, DC, NDU-U.S. National War College, 26 April 1999.

179. For a recent analysis of Power's role see Jacob Heilbrunn, "Samantha and Her Subjects," The National Interest, No. 113, May/June 2011, pp. 6-15.

180. Cooper and Myers, "Obama Takes Hard Line" op. cit.; General Clapper had testified before the Senate Armed Services Committee on March 10, 2011, that

the better-equipped Gaddafi armed forces over the longer term would prevail. Accessible at http://www.cbsnews.com/8301-503544_162-20041688-503544.html.

181. David Jablonsky, "The Persistence of Credibility: Interests, Threats and Planning for the Use of American Military Power," Strategic Review, Spring 1996, pp. 7-15.

182. Anthony J. Mayo and Nitin Nohria, *In Their Time: The Greatest Business Leaders of the 20th Century*, Cambridge: Mass, Harvard Business Press, September 2005.

183. Charles Hill, Grand Strategies, op. cit., p. 257.

184. Barry Rubin, "No Wonder Hillary resigned," The Rubin Report, 18 March, 2011, http://www.Rubinreports.blogspotcom; see also Daniel Henninger, "The Collapse of Internationalism," The Wall Street Journal, March 17, 2011.

185. Barack Obama, *The Audacity of Hope*, New York: Crown Publishers, 2006, p. 302.

186. J. Ann Tickner, *Gender in International Relations Feminist Perspectives on Achieving Global Security*, New York: Columbia University Press, 1992 and Annick T. R. Wibben, "Feminist International Relations: Old Debates and New Directions," Brown Journal of World Affairs, Winter/Spring 2004, Vol. X, Issue 2.

187. Anne-Marie Slaughter, Gayle Smith, James B. Steinberg, Ivo H. Daalder, Susan Rice, et.al. "Strategic Leadership: A Framework for a 21st Century National Security Strategy," Center for a New American Security, Washington, DC, July 2008.

188. James Kitfield, "Libya: Coalition of the Leaderless," National Journal, 21 March, 2011; accessible at http://security.nationaljournal.com/2011/03/libya-coalitionof-the-leaderl.php.

189. "Who's in charge? Germans pull forces out of NATO AS Libyan coalition falls apart," Daily Mail, 23rd March, 2011, p. 1.

190. Steven Metz and Phillip Cuccia, "Defining War For the 21st Century,," SSI Annual Strategy Conference Report, Carlisle: PA, U.S. Army War College, February 2011, p. 12.

191. Charles Hill, Grand Strategies, op. cit., p. 283.

192. Supporters of the new global agenda at Stanford University have initiated a prototypical Program on Liberation Technology: "Lying at the intersection of social science, computer science, and engineering, the Program on Liberation Technology seeks to understand how information technology can be used to defend human rights, improve governance, empower the poor, promote economic development, and pursue a variety of other social goods." See http://liberationtechnology.stanford.edu.

193. Clay Shirky, "The Political Power of Social Media," Foreign Affairs Vol. 90, No. 1, January/February 2011 pp. 31-38.

194. General David Petraeus quoted in J. Robinson West, "We Are Actively 2011; accessible at http://online.wsj.com/article/SB1000142405274870337340457614860 1662888050.html#articleTabs percent3Darticle.

195. Sean Aday, Henry Farrell, Marc Lynch, John Sides, John Kelly and Ethan Zucker-man, "Blogs and Bullets: New Media in Contentious Politics," Peaceworks No. 65, US Institute of Peace, 2010, p. 19.

196. Twitter is a website owned and operated by Twitter Inc., which offers a social networking and micro-blogging service, enabling its users to send and read messages called tweets. Tweets are text-based posts of up to 140 characters dis-played on the user's profile page. Tweets are publicly visible by default. http://en.wikipedia.org/wiki.Twitter.

197. World Report 2010," Human Rights Watch, New York: NY, 2010; accessible at http://www.hrw.org/en/world-report-2010.

198. Shirky, op. cit., p. 4. See also Nikolas Gvosdev "The Realist Prism: Politics vs. Social Media in the Arab Uprising," World Politics Review, March 4, 2011. Accessed on March 4, 2011 at http://www.worldpoliticsreview.com/articles/8089.

199. Ibid., 26.

200. Evgeny Morozov, *The Net Delusion: The Dark Side of Internet Freedom*, New York: Public Affairs, 2011.

201. Evgeny Morozov, "Freedom.gov," Foreign Policy, January/February 2011, pp. 34-35; Clay Shirky, "Netizens Unite," Foreign Policy, March/April 2011, pp. 14-15.

202. Ibid.

203. Shirky, op. cit., p. 41.

204. Nikolas Gvosdev, "The Realist Prism: Politics vs. Social Media in the Arab Upris-ing," World Politics Review, March 4, 2011. Last accessed on March 5, 2011 at http://worldpoliticsreview.com/articles/print/8089.

205. Philip N. Howard, "The digital Origins of dictatorship and Democracy," Pre-sentation at the CDDRL, PGJ, Program on Liberation Technology, Stanford University, March 10, 2011.

206. "Challenges to Dissent Inside China," Stratfor, February 24, 2011; accessible at http://www.stratfor.com/memberships/185854/analysis/20110223-challenges-dissent-inside-china.

207. Adam Entous and Julian E. Barnes, "U.S. Wavers on 'Regime Change,'" The Wall Street Journal, March 5/6, 2011, p. A6.

208. Ibid., A1.

209. Ibid.

210. Praveen Swami, "Saudi Arabian troops sent to Bahrain as protests escalate," The Telegraph, Monday, March 14, 2011; accessible at http://www.telegraph.co.uk/news/worldnews/middleeast/bahrain/8381034/Saudi-Arabian-troops-sent-to-Bahrain-as-protests-escalate.htm.

211. Entour and Barnes, "U.S. Wavers," op. cit.

212. Nikolas Gvosdev, "The Realist Prism: Politics vs. Social Media in the Arab Upris-ing," World Politics Review, March 4, 2011; accessible at http://worldpoliticsre-view.com/articles/print/8089.

213. The war officially stopped with the signing by all Congolese stakeholders of the 2003 Global and Inclusive Agreement on the Transition. See "DDR in the Democratic Republic of Congo: Program Update," World Bank, September 2009; and "Second Congo War," http://www.fact-archive.com/encyclopedia/Second_Congo_War.

214. Daniel Byman, "Terrorism After the Revolution," Foreign Affairs, Volume 90 No. 2, May/June 2011, pp. 48-54.

215. Julian E. Barnes and Adam Entous, "Upheaval in Mideast Sets Back Terror War," The Wall Street Journal, 17 March, 2011, p. A1.

216. Ibid.

217. Ibid.

218. Ibid.

219. Iona Craig, "Yemen president to step down in a month under deal," USA Today, April 26, 2011, p. 1.

220. Mitchell D. Silber and Arvin Blatt, *Radicalization in the West: The Homegrown Threat*, NYPD: NYPD Intelligence Division, 2007. Available at http:/tinyurl.com/2de6qmq.

221. Jeffery S. Barding "Cyber Jihadist Use of the Internet: What can be done?" Intelligencer: Journal of U.S. Intelligence Studies, Vol. 18, No.1,Fall/Winter 2010, p. 31.

222. Nick Fielding and Ian Cobain, "Revealed: US spy operation that manipulates social media," The Guardian, 17 March, 2011; accessible at www.guardian.co.uk/technology.2011/mar/17/us-spy-operation-social-networks/print.

223. Ibid.

224. Ibid.

225. Ibid.

226. Ibid.

227. The White House, "Remarks by the President in Address to the Nation on Libya," 28 March, 2011, www.whitehouse.gov.the-press-office/2011.03/28/remarks-president-address-nation-libya.

228. Joseph P. Nye Jr., *The Paradox of American Power: Why the World's Only Superpower Can't Go It Alone*, New York: Oxford University Press, 2002, p. 176 note #31.

229. Kroenig et.al. "Taking Soft Power Seriously," op. cit.

230. Christopher M. Schnaubelt, "The Illusions and delusions of Smart Power," in Christopher M. Schnaubelt ed. *Towards A Comprehensive Approach: Integrating Civilian and Military Concepts of Strategy*, Rome: Italy, NATO Defense College, 2011, pp. 23-52.

231. H. Gelb, Power Rules, New York: Harper Collins, 2009, p. 39.

232. Samantha Power, "Bystanders to Genocide," The Atlantic, September 2001, accessible at http://www.theatlantic.com/magazine/archive/2001/09/bystanders-to-Devil: *The Failure of Humanity in Rwanda*, New York: Da Capo Press, December 21, 2004.

233. Gelb, Power Rules, op. cit., pp. 40-41.

234. The 2010 Census reported 308,745,538 residents in the U.S., the third largest in the world. Racially, the U.S. has a White American majority. Minorities compose just over one-third of the population (102.5 million in 2007), with Hispanic and Latino Americans and Black Americans as the largest minority groups, by ethnicity and race, respectively. Accessible at http://en.wikipedia.org/wiki/Demographics_of_the_United_States.

235. Gelb, op. cit., p. 41.

236. Colin S. Gray, "Hard Power and Soft Power: The Utility of Military Force As an Instrument of Policy in the 21St Century," Carlisle: PA, Strategic Studies Institute-NDU, April 2011, p. 35.

237. Arthur M. Schesinger, *The Disuniting of America: Reflections on a Multicultural Society*, Revised and enlarged edition, New York: W.W. Norton, 1998.

238. Nicolas Sarkozy joins David Cameron and Angela Merkel view that multiculturalism has failed," Daily Mail, February 11, 2011; accessible at http://www.dailymail.co.uk/news/article-1355961/Nicolas-Sarkozy-joins-David-Cameron-Angela-Merkel-view-multiculturalism-failed.html#ixzz1FctmQFpl.

239. Paula Neuding, "The Cultural Contradictions of Multiculturalism," Project Syndicate, February 24, 2011; accessible at http://www.project-syndicate.org/commentary/neuding1/English.

240. Gelb, op. cit., p. 41.

241. Ibid., 42.

242. "Charismatic Authority," Wikipedia; accessible at http://en.wikipedia.org/wiki/Charismatic_authority#cite_note-0. Max Weber described charisma as "a certain quality of an individual personality, by virtue of which he is set apart from ordinary men and treated as endowed with supernatural, superhuman, or at least specifically exceptional qualities or powers" Maximillan. Weber, "The Nature of Charismatic Authority and its Routinization" in Theory of Social and Economic Organization, translated by A. R. Anderson and Talcott Parsons in 1947 was originally published in 1922 in German under the title *Wirtschaft und Gesellschaft* and is available online in German at http://www.textlog.de/7415.html.

243. Gelb, op. cit., p. 42.

244. Angelo M. Codevilla, "Tools of Statecraft: Diplomacy and War," Foreign Policy Research Institute, January 2008; accessible athttp://www.fpri.org/footnotes/1301.200801.codevilla.statecraftdiplomacywar.html.

245. Ibid.

246. http://globalr2p.org/media/pdf/UNResolutionA63L.80Rev.1.pdf.

247. Mark Knoller, "National Debt to Top 100 percent of GDP," CBSnews.com, 23 July 2010; accessible at www.cbsnews.com/8301-503544_162-20011546-503544.html.

248. During the Reagan years the defense budget peaked at 6 .2 percent of GDP while the baseline defense budget as of first quarter 2011 is currently at 3.6 percent of GDP. In fact, the active-duty military is two-thirds its size during the 1980s.

249. Paul McLeary, "The Failed History of the QDR," Aviation Week, September 4, 2009; accessible at http://www.aviationweek.com/aw/blogs/defense/.

250. Tom Donnelly, "Kill the QDR," AFJ-Armed Forces Journal, February 1, 2006, accessible at http://www.armedforcesjournal.com/2006/02/1813832.

251. Roy Godson and Richard H. Shultz, Jr., "The Pentagon is not Preparing for the Most Likely Conflicts, Small Wars Foundation," 2010; last accessed on November 14, 2010 at http://smallwarsjournal.com/blog/journal/docs-temp/496-godson.pdf.

252. Robert M. Gates, "A Balanced U.S. Military Strategy," Vol. 88, No. 1 Foreign Affairs, January/February 2009, p. 28.

253. Thomas G. Manhnken, "Striving for Balance in Defense," Proceedings Magazine, U.S. Naval Institute, June 2010, Vol.136/6/1, p. 288.

254. Ibid.

255. A.C. Brooks, E.J. Feulner and W. Kristol, "Peace Doesn't Keep Itself," Wall Street Journal, October 4, 2010, p. A 25.

256. Joint Statement of William J. Perry and Stephen J. Hadley Before the House Armed Services Committee, on the "Quadrennial Defense Review Independent Panel," Washington, DC, 29 July 2010; accessible at www.usip.org.

257. Joint Statement of Perry and Hadley, op. cit.

258. Ibid.

259. Ibid.

260. Micah Zenko, Between Threats and War: U.S. Discrete Military Operations in the Post-Cold War World, Palo Alto: CA, Stanford University Press, 2010.

261. The official title of the SOFA is "Agreement Between the United States of America and the Republic of Iraq On the Withdrawal of United States Forces from Iraq and the Organization of Their Activities during Their Temporary Presence in Iraq" http://en.wikipedia.org/wiki/U.S.percentE2percent80percent93Iraq_Status_of_Forces_Agreement.

262. Rep. Jason Chaffetz (UT) chairman, U.S. House of Representatives Oversight and Government Reform Subcommittee on National Security, Homeland Defense & Foreign Operations, Opening Remarks, "U.S. Military Leaving Iraq: Is the State Department Ready?," Public Hearing, March 2, 2011.

263. Admiral Mike Mullen, "The Proper Use of the Military," Aviation Week and Space Technology, March 22, 2010; Landon Lecture Series Address, Kansas State University, Wednesday, March 3, 2010 www.jcs.mil/speech.aspx?ID=1336.

264. Admiral Eric. T. Olson, "A Balanced Approach to Irregular Warfare," The Journal of International Security Affairs, Spring 2009, No. 16; last accessed June 5, 2010 at www.securityaffairs.org/issues/2009/16/olson.php.

265. Mr. X, "A National Strategic Narrative," Princeton: New Jersey, Woodrow Wilson International Center for Scholars, 2011.

266. Bruce Russett, *Controlling the Sword*, Cambridge: Mass. Harvard University Press, 1990.

267. Peter D. Feaver, "The Right to Be Right: Civil-Military Relations and the Iraq Surge Decision," International Security, Vol. 35, No.4, (Spring 2011), p. 93.

268. Ibid., 89.

269. Ibid., 90.

270. Michael J. Carden "McChrystal Retires Amid Praise for Career," American Forces Press Service, DOD, 23 July , 2010. Accessible at http://www.defense.gov./news/newsarticle.aspx?id=60157.

271. Ibid.

272. Michael Hastings, "The Runaway General," Rolling Stone, June 22, 2010 accessed at www.rollingstone.com/politics/news/the-runaway-general-20100622 See also "Top 2 Civilians Face Rockiness in Afghan Shift," The New York Times, Thursday, July 1, 2010, p. A1. In an interesting twist, soon thereafter some recommended that McChrystal be put in charge of overseeing the troop drawdown in Iraq. See Christopher Hitchens "One More Mission" Slate, 5 July , 2010; accessible at www.slate.com/2259431.

273. The Washington Post, "Pentagon Worries Led to Command Change," August 17, 2009; last accessed on Aug. 4, 2010 at www.washingtonpost.com/wp-dyn/content/article/2009/08/16/AR2009081602304.html.

274. Fred Kaplan, "McChrystal: Gone and Soon Forgotten," Slate, 23 June, 2010. Accessible at www.slate.com/id/2257956/pagenum/all.

275. Samuel P. Huntington's classic *The Soldier and the State: The Theory and Politics of Civil-Military Relations*, New York: NY, Belknap Press, 1957.

276. Thom Shanker, "Gates Tightens Rules for Military and the Media," The New York Times, July 2, 2010 at www.nytimes.com/2010/07/03/world/03pentagon.html?_r=1&partner=rssnyt&emc=rss. See also "Military officials will need OK before nterviews," accessible at http://news.yahoo.com/s/ap/20100703/ap_on_go_ca_st_pe/us_gates_media_rules. (Last accessed on Sat. Jul 3, 2010).

277. Celeste Ward Guenter, "Why US soldiers in Afghanistan are so frustrated," The Christian Science Monitor, June 30, 2010, accessed on January 12, 2011 at http://www.csmonitor.com/Commentary/Opinion/2010/0630/Why-US-soldiers-in-Afghanistan-are-so-frustrated.

278. See Rod Norland, "U.N. Reports Rising Afghan Casualties" The New York Times, August 10, 2010 www.nytimes.com/2010/08/11/world/asia/11afghan.html?_r=1&hp.

279. Ibid.

280. Hugh Gusterson, "Against counterinsurgency in Afghanistan," Bulletin of the Atomic Scientists, July 1, 2010. Accessible at http://thebulletin.org/web-edition/columnists/hugh-gusterson/against-counterinsurgency-afghanistan.

281. James M. Dorsey, "U.S. Counterterrorism Strategy Boomerangs in Yemen, Somalia," World Politics Review, October 26, 2010; accessed on 10/27/2010 at www.worldpoliticsreview.com articles/6826/u-s-counterterrorism-strategy-boomerangs-in-yemen-somalia.

282. Gary T. Dempsey, "Old Folly in a New Disguise: Nation-Building to Combat Terrorism," Policy Analysis No. 429, Cato Institute, March 21, 2002.

283. For a political analysis of the Bush administration decision making during the surge debates see Peter D. Feaver, op. cit., pp. 87-125.

284. John A. Nagl, Foreword, "The Evolution and Importance of Army/Marine Corps Field Manual 3-24, Counterinsurgency in The U.S. Army/Marine Corps Counterinsurgency Field Manual, Chicago, Ill, U of Chicago Press, 2007. David Galula (1919-1967) was a French military officer and scholar who wrote books about counterinsurgency in Indochina, Greece, and Algeria. He served as a military attaché in China but did not participate in the Indochina war.

285. Joint Publication (JP), Department of Defense Dictionary of Military and Associated Terms, April 2001 (as amended through 31 October 2009) and available at www.dtic.mil/doctrine/new_pubs/jp1_02pdf.

286. Jim Garamonte, "Iraqi Surge Was Keystone to Iraq," The New York Times 11 September, 2008; accessible at http://www.nyjtimes.com/cover/09-11-08/Iraqi-SurgeWasKeystone.htm.

287. Kimberly Kagan, The Surge: A Military History, New York: Encounter Books, 2008.

288. Thomas E. Ricks, "Iraq: The Unraveling?," Foreign Policy, 30 March 2009, accessible at http://ricks.foreignpolicy.com/posts/2009/03/30/iraq-the_unraveling.

289. Lee Hamilton as quoted in David Corn, "Petraeus and the Myth of the Surge," Mother Jones, 23 June, 2010, accessible at http://motherjones.com/mojo/ 2010/06/ petraeus-surge-afghanistan-iraq.

290. Ibid.

291. Robert M. Gates, "A Balanced Strategy," op. cit., p. 28.

292. Gian Gentile "Exposing Counterfeit COIN," accessed on Feb. 16, 2011 at http://original.antiwar.com/vlahos/2009/05/06/gian-gentile-exposing-counterfeit-coin/.

293. Michael S. Child, Sr. "Memorandum for the Inspector General, Department of the Army," Inspector General Department of Defense, Foreign Policy, April 8, 2011; accessed at www.foreignpolicy.com/files/fp_uploaded_documents/110419_ ROI508.pdf.

294. Stanley A. McChrystal, "Becoming the Enemy" Foreign Policy, March/April 2011, pp. 66-70.

295. Ibid., 67.

296. Ibid., 68.

297. Ibid., 69.

298. Ibid., 69.

299. Ibid.

300. Ibid.

301. Ibid.

302. Bob Woodward, "Why Did the Violence Plummet? It Wasn't Just the Surge," The Washington Post, September 8, 2008.

303. John Arquilla and David Ronfeldt, "Networks and Netwars: the future of terror, crime, and militancy," Santa Monica, CA, RAND Corp., 2001. On swarming see Sean Edwards, "Swarming on the Battlefield," Santa Monica: CA, RAND Corp., 2000.

304. Christopher J. Lamb and Evan Munsing, "Secret Weapon: High Value Target Teams as an Organizational Innovation," Strategic Perspectives #4, INSS-NDU, March 2011, p.28.

305. Ibid., 3.

306. McChrystal, "Becoming the Enemy," op. cit.

307. Jeremy Scahill, "The Secret US War in Pakistan," The Nation, 7 December, 2009.

308. Julius Cavendish, "US Military offers sheep in apology for Afghanistan deaths," The Christian Science Monitor, 8 April 2010; Spencer Ackerman, "McChrystal Consolidates Control of Special Forces in Afghanistan," 16 March, 2010 http://washington independent.com/79343/mcchrystal-consolidates-control-of-special-forces-in-afghanistan.

309. Dov Zakheim, "What can we expect from James Mattis," Shadow Government, July 12, 2010; at http://shadow.foreignpolicy.com/category/topic/afghanistan?page=1.

310. Joint Publication 1-02, p. 130.

311. Interview in "Today" on NBC, Thursday July 29, 2010.

312. Patrick B. Johnston, "Assessing the Effectiveness of Leadership Decapitation in Counterinsurgency Campaigns." In 11th Annual Triangle Institute for Security Studies New Faces Conference. Chapel Hill, NC, October, 2010, p. 29.

313. Helen Cooper and Mark Landler, "Targeted Killing is new US focus in Afghanistan," The New York Times, July 31, 2010; last accessed on August 1, 2010 at www.nytimes.com/2010/08/01/world/asia/01afghan.html.

314. www.usacac.army.mil/blog/blogs/coin/archive/2010/08/02/general-petraeusis-sues-new-comisaf-coin-guidance.aspx.

315. Ibid.

316. "U.S. Military Seeks Slower Pace to Wrap Up Afghan Role," The New York Times, August 11, 2010; accessible at www.nytimes.com/2010/08/12/world/asia/12policy.html?_r=2&pagewanted=1&hpw.

317. Ibid.

318. Daniel Dombey and Matthew Green "US troops set for longer Afghan stay" FT.COM, February 17, 2011. http://www.ft.com/cms/s/0/a89214ac-3ac4-11e0-9c1a-00144feabdc0.html#axzz1ELRnOmgK.

319. NATO Afghan exit could mean civil war, Kandaharis say," Reuters, Nov. 28, 2010; accessible at http://www.abs-cbnnews.com/global-filipino/world/11/28/10/nato-afghan-exit-could-mean-civil-war-kandaharis-say.

320. "Clear, hold, hand over," IISS, op. cit.

321. Statement of General David H. Petraeus, U.S. Army Commander, International Security Assistance Forces NATO Before the Senate Armed Services Committee, 15 Mar 2011, p. 3.

322. Matthew Rosenberg and Julian E. Barnes, "Al Qaeda Makes Afghan Comeback," The Wall Street Journal, April 6, 2011, p. 1.

323. On the DOD permissible ROEs on drugs see James Rissen, State of War, New York: Free Press, 2006, p. 157.

324. Peter L. Bergen, The Longest War, op. cit., p. 179.

325. Maria Abi-Habib, "Karzai to Replace Two U.S.-Favored Ministers," The Wall Street Journal, Friday, April 8, 2011, p. A7.

326. U.S. Senate, Committee on Armed Services, 15 March, 2011, Archived Webcast, accessible at http://armed-services.senate.gov/e_witnesslist.cfm?id=5058.

327. Michael Few, "The Wrong War: An Interview with Bing West," Small Wars Journal, February 21, 2011.

328. Bing West, The Wrong War: Grit, Strategy, and the Way Out of Afghanistan, New York: Random House, 2011.

329. Andrew Exum, "In Afghanistan With Our Warrior Elite," The Wall Street Journal, February 19, 2011.

330. Dan Balz and Bob Woodward, "America's Chaotic Road to War," The Washington Post, Sunday, January 27, 2002, p. A01.

331. The Solarium results were presented by each team on July 16th, 1953, at a special meeting of the NSC with the Joint Chiefs of Staff, the NSC Planning Board, and the Service Secretaries. After listening to each presentation, Eisenhower himself summarized and commented on each and all of them before announcing his preference for the findings of team A. He ordered the NSC Planning Board to integrate common features of the three presentations and recommend actions needed for immediate implementation. The result was NSC-162/2—the institutionalization of the Truman-Kennan policy of containment. See William B. Pickett, editor, George F. Kennan and the Origins of Eisenhower's New Look, Princeton Institute for International and Regional Studies, Princeton University, 2004, accessible at http://www.rose-hulman.edu/~pickett/Solarium.pdf; See also Project Solarium, http://www.eisenhowermemorial.org/stories/Project-Solarium.htm.

332. Ernest R. May, ed. American Cold War Strategy: Interpreting NSC-68, New York: St. Martin's Press, 1993.

333. Michele A. Flournoy and Shawn W. Brinley, "Strategic Planning for U.S. National Security: A Project Solarium for the 21st Century, The Princeton Project Paper, 2006 accessible at www.princeton.edu/~ppns/papers/interagencyQNSR.pdf.

334. Ibid., 4.

335. Ibid.

336. Ibid., 10.

337. Ibid., 14-17.

338. Tyler Nottberg, "Once and Future Policy Planning: Solarium for Today," The Eisenhower Institute, accessible at http://www.eisenhowerinstitute.org/about/living_history/solarium_for_today.dot.

339. John S.D. Eisenhower, *General Ike: A Personal Reminiscence*, New York: Free Press of Simon & Schuster, 2003. Operation Barbarossa, the Nazi invasion of the Soviet Union that began on 22 June, 1941, was the largest military operation in human history.

340. "The Military-Industrial Complex at 50: Assessing the Meaning and Impact of Eisenhower's Farewell Address: Panel 1. The Wars Within: Thoughts on the State of Civil–Military Relations" in 2011, Cato Institute, Washington, DC, January 13, 2011; htpp://www.cato.org/event.php?eventid=7604.

341. President Obama said McChrystal's conduct "undermines the civilian control of the military ... " Robert Burns, "Pentagon probe clears Gen. McChrystal," San Francisco Chronicle, April 19, 2011, p. A4.

342. Leon Mangasarian and Viola Gienger, "U.S. Says Libyan Campaign to Ease as No-Fly Zone Is Secured," Bloomberg, 22 March, 2011; accessible at www.bloomberg.com/news/2011-03-22/allies-control-of-airspace-in-libya-putsqaddafi-s-ground-forces-at-risk.htm. Secretary Gates was in an official visit to Moscow when he made his remarks.

343. Gates, Landon Lecture, op. cit.

344. Hans Binneendijk and Patrick M. Cronin, ed. "Civilian Surge: Key to Complex Operations," Center for Technology and National Policy, National Defense University, Washington: DC, 2009, p. 5.

345. Secretary of State Condoleezza Rice, "Remarks on Transformational Diplomacy," January 18, 2006, Washington: DC Georgetown University in Justin Vaisse "Transformational Diplomacy," Chaillot Paper, No. 103, Paris: France, European Union Institute for Security Studies, June 2007, Annex A.

346. Admiral Mullen retired 30 September 2011, replaced by General Martin E. Dempsey.

347. Lisa Daniel, "Gates: U.S. Must Consider Sustainability of Afghan Forces," American Forces Press Service, February 17, 2011 accessible at http://www.defense.gov/news/newsarticle.aspx?id=62857.

348. Robert M. Gates, Secretary of Defense, "A Balanced Strategy: Reprogramming The Pentagon For a New Age," Foreign Affairs, January 2009 and Hillary Rodham Clinton, Secretary of State, Testimony before the Senate Appropriations Committee, Washington , DC, April 2009.

349. The First Quadrennial Diplomacy and Development Review (QDDR): Leading Through Civilian Power, U.S. Department of State, December 2010; accessible at http://www.state.gov/documents/organization/153142.pdf.

350. Ibid.

351. Her full resume is at www.princeton.edu/~slaughtr/Admin/SlaughterCV2.pdf.

352. David E. Sanger and Thom Shanker, "Obama is Set To Redo Team on War Policy," The New York Times, 7 April 2011, p. A1.

353. This section draws heavily from the CRS Report for Congress, "U.S. Special Operations Forces (SOF); Background and Issues for Congress," by Andrew Feickert and Thomas K. Livingston, CRS 7-5700, RS21048, March 28, 2011.

354. 10 U. S. Code, Sect.167 (a).

355. USSOCOM accessible at www.socom.mil/SOCOMHome/Pages/USSOCOM.aspx.

356. Col. David Gurney and Dr. Jeffrey D. Smotherman, "An Interview with Eric T. Olson," Joint Forces Quarterly, Issue 56, 1st quarter 2010.

357. Posture Statement of Admiral Eric T. Olson, USN Commander United States Special Operations Command," before the 112th Congress, Senate Armed Services Committee, March 1, 2011.

358. Charles G. Cogan, "Desert One and Its Disorders," The Journal of Military History Vol. 67 No. 1, 2003, pp. 201-216.

359. http://en.wikipedia.org/wiki/Office_of_Strategic_Services.

360. Admiral Eric Olson, "USSOCOM: Function and Focus," Center for Strategic and International Studies (CSIS), Transcript by Federal News Service, Washington, DC, April 1, 2010, p. 3.

361. Mr. Gearing, "The Chairman's Joint Training System," Horizons, Issue 4, Summer, 2011, p. 31.

362. Olson, CSIS, op. cit.

363. Ibid.

364. "An Interview with Eric T. Olson," op. cit.

365. DODD 3000.07, December 1, 2008; accessible at http://www.dtic.mil/. whs/directives/corres/pdf/300007p.pdf.

366. Posture Statement of Admiral Eric T. Olson, 112th Congress, Senate Armed Services Committee, March 1, 2011.

367. Admiral Eric T. Olson, Speech on 3 March 2008 delivered at the Willard Hotel, Washington, DC.

368. Ibid.

369. Testimony of Michael G. Vickers, "SOCOM'S Missions and Roles," U.S. House of Representatives, Committee on Armed Services, Subcommittee on Terrorism, Unconventional Threats, and Capabilities, June 29, 2006.

370. Olson, "2011Posture Statement," op. cit.

371. Admiral Eric Olson, "USSOCOM: Function and Focus," Center for Strategic and International Studies (CSIS), Transcript by Federal News Service, Washington, DC, April 1, 2010.

372. Michele Malvesti, "USSOCOM: Function and Focus," CSIS, Ibid.

373. Mike Ryan, The Operators: Inside the World's Special Forces, New York: Skyhorse Publishing, 2008, p. 205.

374. Michele L. Malvesti, "To Serve the Nation: U.S. Special Operation Forces in an Era of Persistent Conflict." Center for a New American Security," Washington, DC, June 2010.

375. Lieutenant Colonel (retired) Roger D. Carstens, U.S. Army Special Forces, "Special Operations Forces: Challenges and Opportunities," Testimony Before the House Armed Services Committee's Subcommittee on Terrorism and Unconventional Threats and Capabilities, U.S. House of Representatives, 3 March 2009, p. 14.

376. Olson, CSIS, April 1, 2010, op. cit.

377. Malvesti, op. cit.

378. Ibid.

379. The original author of the SOF Truths was retired Army Colonel John M. Collins who as a Congressional Research Service analyst wrote "United States and Soviet Special Operations," CRS-Library of Congress, April 28, 1987, Washington: DC U.S.G.P.O. 87-271-P. For a history see www.shadowspear.com/vb/threads/5th-sof-truth-added-re-inserted.4748.

380. Department of Defense, Quadrennial Defense Review Report, February 2010.

381. Olson, CSIS, op. cit., pp. 5-6.

382. Joint Publication 1-02, DOD Dictionary of Military and Associated Terms 12 April 2001, as amended through 16 October 2006.

383. Testimony before the House Armed Services Committee, September 22, 2011.

384. Olson, "USSOCOM; Functions and Focus," CSIS, op. cit.

385. USSOCOM, Limited Objective Experiment (LOE) 13-16 July 2010, p. 68.

386. Admiral Eric T. Olson, "A Balanced Approach to Irregular Warfare," The Journal of International Security Affairs, Spring 2009, No. 16.

387. Admiral Eric T. Olson, "USSOCOM: Function and Focus," CSIS, op. cit.

388. Testimony before the House Armed Services Committee, op. cit.

389. Section 1208 of P.L. 108-375, the FY 2005 National Defense Authorization Act.

390. Olson, "A Balanced Approach," op. cit.

391. Admiral Eric T. Olson, Commander USSOCOM, 2010 Posture Statement, House Appropriations Committee Subcommittee on Defense, HAC-D, 18 June 2010.

392. Major General Michael T. Flynn, Capt. Matt Pottinger and Paul D. Batchelor, "Fixing Intelligence: a Blueprint for Making Intelligence Relevant in Afghanistan," CNAS, Washington, DC , January 2010.

393. USSOCOM, Research Topics 2011, MacDill Air Force Base, Tampa: Fla., Joint Special Operations University.

394. Basil Henry Liddell Hart, The Strategy of the Indirect Approach, London: UK, Faber and Faber Limited, Digital publication 5/19/25. http://www.archive.org/details/strategyofindire035126mb.

395. B. H. Liddell Hart, Strategy, New York: Praeger Publishers, 1967; Signet Books, 1974, p. 352.

396. B. H. Liddell Hart, *Strategy: The Indirect Approach*, New York: Praeger, 1954, p. 339.

397. Ralph D. Sawyer, *The Complete Art of War: Sun Tzu*, Colorado: Westview Press, 1996.

398. Ibid., 15-36.

399. Bennet Sacolick, "What's so Special About Special Forces?" available at www.sfa20.org/Documents/Whats percent20so percent20special percent20about percent20SF.pdf.

400. Ibid.

401. Thomas H. Henriksen, *Afghanistan, Counterinsurgency, and the Indirect Approach*, JSOU-Report 10-3, JSOU Press, 2010.

402. Eric T. Olson, CSIS, op. cit.

403. Michelle Malvesti, CSIS, op. cit.

404. See Dena Montague and Frida Berrigan, "The Business of War in the Democratic Republic of Congo", *Dollars and Sense* magazine, July/August 2001, reproduced in Third World Traveler at www.thirdworldtraveler.com/Africa/Business_War_Congo.html.

405. The DRC's Country Assistance Framework: A 'Big Tent' built from 'Big Ideas'?" Joint UN-Bank Review of the DRC CAF, United Nations Department of Peacekeeping Operations (DPKO); The World Bank Group, 30 May 2008.

406. Principal Deputy Assistant Secretary of State Donald Yamamoto, Testimony before the House Foreign Affairs Committee Subcommittee on Africa, Global Health, and Human Rights, March 8, 2011; accessible at http://www.internationalrelations.house.gov/112/yam030811.

407. Ibid.

408. "UN officials calls Congo 'rape capital of the world'" BBC NEWS, 28 April 2010, accessible at htpp://news.bbc.co.uk/ /2/hi/8650112.stm.

409. Nicole Dalrymple, "U.S. and DRC in partnership to train model Congolese battalion," www.army.mil, February 18, 2010.

410. Ibid.

411. David Axe, "The Limits of Smart Power," The American Prospect, November 29, 2010; accessible at www.prospect.org/cs/articles?article= the_limits_of_smart_power.

412. Ibid.

413. U.S. Department of State, "Trafficking in Persons Report, 2010"; accessible at www.state.gov/g/tip/rls/tiprpt/2010/142747.htm.

414. During the Libyan revolt the USS Kearsarge, OCP's main vessel, was dispatched to the Mediterranean to provide humanitarian relief in the rebel-held Eastern part of the country.

415. "48 Women Raped Every Hour in Congo, Study Finds," The Associated Press (AP), 11 May, 2011.

416. Nathan Hodge, *Armed Humanitarians: The Rise of the Nation Builders*, New York: Bloomsbury, 2011.

417. Michel G. Roskin, National Interest: From Abstraction to Strategy, Carlisle, PA: Strategic Studies Institute, 1994, p. 16.

418. Michael Mandelbaum, "Foreign Policy as Social Work," Foreign Affairs, Vol. 75, No.1, 1996, pp. 16-32.

419. Coit D. Blacker, The New Global Agenda, op. cit.

420. James Kinnigburgh and Dorothy Denning, Blogs and Military Information Strategy, JSOU Report 06-5 Hurlburt Field: Fl, The JSOU Press, June 2006.

421. Author's conversation with Admiral Olson during "Sovereign Challenge VI Conference," El Paso, Texas, November 9, 2010.

422. Jeff McKaughan, "Q & A: Lieutenant General David P. Fridovich," SOTECH, Volume 8 Issue 4, June 2010.

423. Michelle L. Malvesti, "To Serve the Nation: U.S. Special Operations Forces in an Era of Persistent Conflict," Center for a New American Security, June 2010.

424. Sean D. Naylor, "Support grows for standing up an unconventional warfare command," Armed Forces Journal, September2007; accessible at www.armed-forcesjournal.com/2007/09/3049653.

425. David Tucker and Christopher J. Lamb, "Restructuring Special Operations Forces for Emerging Threats," Strategic Forum, Institute for National Strategic Studies, No. 219, January 2006. pp. 1-6. See also their book length elaboration David Tucker and Christopher J. Lamb, United States Special Operations Forces, New York: Columbia University Press, 2007.

426. Ibid., 3.

427. Naylor, op. cit.

428. Admiral Eric T. Olson, 2010 Posture Statement, p. 5.

429. Admiral Eric T. Olson, Testimony before the U.S. Senate Subcommittee on Emerging Threats and Capabilities, Committee on Armed Services, Washington, DC, June 18, 2009.

430. Posture Statement of Admiral Eric T. Olson, Before the 112th Congress, Senate Armed Services Committee, March 1, 2011.

431. Written testimony of Vice Admiral William H. McRaven, USN Commander Designate, USSOCOM to the Senate Armed Services Committee, June 28, 2011, pp. 18-19.

432. Admiral Michael Mullen, USN, Chairman of the Joint Chiefs of Staff, Hearing of the Senate Armed Services Committee, Federal News Service, Washington, DC, February 2, 2010.

433. Karen Parrish, "SOF focus on world's 'unlit spaces,'" USSOCOM, www.socom.mil/SOCOMHome/newspub/news/Pages/Specialoperationsunlitspaces.aspx.

434. Major Paul Edwards, "Making Soldiers and Small Units More Decisive," TRADOC Public Affairs, 25 February 2011; accessible at www.army.mil/-news/2011/03/01/52609-making-soldiers-and-small-units-more-decisive/.

435. "Interview with Dr. Malcolm Ross O'Neill," Assistant Secretary of the Army for Acquisition, Logistics and Technology, Army AL & T, January-March 2011, p. 3.

436. Major Paul Edwards, op. cit.

437. Ibid.

438. Bennet Sacolick, "SOF vs. SOF-like," Small Wars Journal, 30 April 2009; available at http:// smallwarsjournal.com/blog/2009/04/sof-vs-SOF-like/.

439. Ibid.

440. Speech by then U.S. Assistant Secretary of Defense Michael Vickers, "Building the Global Counterterrorism Network," The Washington Institute for Near East Policy, Washington: DC, October 24, 2008.

441. Ann Scott Tyson, "Sorry, Charlie, this is Michael Vickers' War," The Washington Post, 28 December, 2007.

442. James D. Kiras, *Special Operations and Strategy*, New York: Routledge, 2006, p. 113.

443. Ibid.

444. Ibid., 114.

445. Ibid., 117.

446. Rachel Martin, "Will Bin Laden's Death Affect Afghan Insurgency?," NPR Morning Edition, May 12, 2011; accessible at http://www.cnas.org/node/6349.

447. Ibid.

448. Anton K. Smith, "Turning on the DIME: Diplomacy's Role in National Security," Carlisle: PA, Strategic Studies Institute, U. S. Army War College, October 12, 2007.

449. Jessica G. Turnley, *Cross-Cultural Competence and Small Groups: Why SOF are the way SOF are*, JSOU Report 11-1, March 2011, JSOU Press, p. 45.

450. Henriksen, *Afghanistan, Counterinsurgency, and the Indirect Approach*, op. cit.

451. Andrew Feickert, "U.S. Special Operations Forces (SOF) Background and Issues for Congress," CRS 7-5700, Report RS21048, July 15, 2011, pp. 8-10.

452. Richard Haass, president of the Council on Foreign Relations called Afghanistan a "strategic distraction" ("Let's Un-Surge in Afghanistan," The Wall Street Journal, December 20, 2010). He later called Libya another "strategic distraction" ("Let's Keep out of Libya," The Wall Street Journal, March 8, 2011).

453. Nathan Hodge, *Armed Humanitarians: The Rise of the Nation Builders*, New York: Bloomsbury, 2011.

454. Bing West, "The Way Out of Afghanistan," Military Review, March/April 2011, pp. 89-95.

455. Linda Robinson, *Tell Me How This Ends: General David Petraeus and the Search for a Way Out of Iraq*, New York: Public Affairs, 2008.

456. Noel M. Tichy and Warren G. Bennis, *Judgement: How Winning Leaders Make Great Calls*, New York: Penguin, 2007, p. 5.

457. Richard H. Shultz Jr, "Showstoppers: Nine reasons why we never sent our Special Operations Forces after al-qaeda before 9/11" The Weekly Standard, January 26, 2004, Vol. 9. N0. 19; last accessed on May 15, 2011 at http://www.weeklystandard.com/Content/Public/Articles/000/000/003/613twavk.asp?page=3.

458. Noel M. Tichy and Warren G. Bennis, *Judgment: How Winning Leaders Make Great Calls*, New York: NY, Penguin Group, 2007, p. 369.

459. Pragmatism as a philosophical movement began in the United States in the 1870s. Its overall direction was determined by the thought and works of Charles Sanders Peirce William James, and Chauncey Wright (members of The Metaphysical Club) as well as John Dewey and George Herbert Mead. See http://en.wikipedia.org/wiki/Pragmatism.

460. John Cecil Masterman, *The Double-Cross System in the War of 1939 to 1945*, Australian National University Press, 1972.

461. Sir William Stephenson, *A Man Called Intrepid*, New York: Ballantine Books, 1978.

462. John Earl Haynes and Harvey Klehr, *Venona*, Yale University Press, 1999.

463. Harry R. Yarger, "How Do Students Learn Strategy?", op. cit.

464. Mr. Y, "A National Strategic Narrative," Woodrow Wilson International Center for Scholars, Washington, DC 2011.

465. Ibid., 5.

466. Joseph S. Nye, Jr. "The War on Soft Power," Foreign Policy, April 12, 2011.

467. Mr. Y, op. cit., p. 10.

468. Michelle Malvesti, "USSOCOM," CSIS, op. cit.

469. For a modern analysis see Barry Strauss, *The Trojan War: A New History*, New York, Simon and Schuster, 1st ed., 2006.

www.ingramcontent.com/pod-product-compliance
Lightning Source LLC
Chambersburg PA
CBHW070707290526
45790CB00001B/486